MW00823677

ASSUME NOTHING

Using Transformational Conversation to
Overcome Unconscious Bias

KIM STEPHENS

Assume Nothing

Using Transformational Conversation to Overcome Unconscious Bias

print ISBN: 978-1-66783-702-4
ebook ISBN: 978-1-66783-703-1

CONTENTS

NOTE: I intentionally used the plural form of pronouns to be more inclusive of all gender identities.

CHAPTER 1.

INTRODUCTION

Goal: Make the reader aware of unconscious bias.

"I'm out in the parking lot, and I'm walking in by myself, and there is um, there's uh, another young man coming in—Black guy, long dreadlocks, a big strong-looking guy, real young. And we're walking in and initially, you know, kind of like, you know, when you're walking, 'Okay. There's a person. There is a person there. Okay, no big deal.' And then he keeps looking at me, you know? So now it's like [making radar sound] 'beep, beep . . .' [laughing] Why, why is he looking at me?"

"And he walks over and says, 'Hey, do I, do I know you?' and I'm looking at him like, 'I don't think so.' I slowed down, and then he stopped. So, I kept walking, and he said, 'No, really, really, I know you.' So, I stopped, and I was like, 'I really don't think you do. I don't recognize you.' Now I'm getting . . . I'm getting scared. I, you know, my initial fight or flight thought was like starting to kick in . . ."

What are your thoughts on what you just read? Are you surprised? Do you identify with the speaker or the unidentified young man? Have you experienced a similar situation? Or perhaps you have been on the receiving end of such a situation. Either way, it is likely your feelings are coupled with some uncomfortableness.

The speaker ends his story by saying that the young man turned out to be a former neighbor who had grown up, so he did not recognize him.

Intro to unconscious bias

In the story above, the speaker was taking the information he had—the man's appearance and the context of the situation—and quickly processing it for a fear response. He may not have realized that in his past he had created a category in his brain with a qualifier—a tall, Black man is frightening. But unconsciously, his brain made a calculation and radioed back to his conscious thinking that he should be wary and afraid. This is an example of unconscious bias.

Research tells us that every second we are exposed to eleven million bits of data. Information comes in from our eyes—what we see, from our ears—what we hear, from our nose—what we smell, etc. All that information bombards us. But out of that eleven million, we can only consciously absorb about forty. And we may be aware of as few as seven.[1] These eleven million bits of data are being processed by our brain as it tries to determine what you need to take in, what you need to react to, and what actions you need to take. This quick processing leads to unconscious bias.

We should first think about what a bias is—a preference, preconceived opinion, inclination, or prejudice. Unconscious biases are biases hidden from a person's conscious awareness. They are processed "behind the scenes." These are seemingly involuntary and affect decision making and behavior. Unconscious biases have developed from a lifetime of experiences that influence how we react to situations, people, places, and everything around us.

Through interactions with others, we create a mind map of assumptions about race, gender, socio-economic status, etc. Each time we encounter a new person, we unconsciously pull out this mind map to see what associations we have already constructed based on characteristics the person presents—making a connection between the person and "a person like them." We categorize and put people into groups that we understand or have experience with—such as white, Black, Asian, Latinx; young or old; boy or girl. These categories allow us to take the unknown and make it familiar.

Categorization also allows quick navigation through the complex world by making associations of "good" or "bad." This categorization isn't always problematic. Unconscious bias most likely developed as an evolutionary safety feature, so that we could quickly determine whether a person was a friend or foe: "Is this person dangerous? What can my past teach me about what I can expect from this person?" We can make quick decisions, and sometimes that is necessary—like knowing to run if you hear gunshots or removing your hand from a hot stove. These are survival mechanisms garnered from our past experiences and applied to our current decision making, but they are also biases that influence our behavior.

In Thinking Fast and Slow, Daniel Kahneman breaks this functioning of your brain into two parts: System 1 and System 2. System 1 is the fast, automatic, and heavy lifter in our brain[2] (2011, pp. 29–30). "System 1 operates automatically and quickly, with little or no effort and no sense of voluntary control."[3] System 2 is the slow and thoughtful part of our brain. Kahneman says that System 2 "allocates attention to the effortful mental activities that demand it, including complex computations. The operations of System 2 are often associated with the subjective experience of agency, choice, and concentration."[4]

So, with eleven million bits of data coming in every second, we, as humans, rely on our System 1 and System 2 to make the right call on what to recognize and whether we will process this information quickly with System 1 or slowly with System 2. Everyone around us is going through this process every second. Thinking about this, it easy to see how each person's perspective can be very different—the human experience and perspective is shaped by whatever forty pieces of data are chosen and how the brain processes this information. As a result, the chances of two people selecting the same data and having the same experience is .00036364 percent. This slim possibility is important because the selection of data—based on our own unconscious biases—influences real-world decisions.

Much of the time, System 1 is very efficient, and we process information accurately and make good decisions. However, in some instances we rely too heavily on System 1. Kahneman describes System 2 as lazy, so we must specifically slow down and consciously call System 2 into our decision-making process. The problem arises when we do not call System 2 when we need it, and we give way to the biases of System 1.

In many cases, there is an urgent need to uncover these unconscious biases and take action to offset their effects. Research suggests that unconscious biases are linked to discriminatory outcomes from poorer quality interactions,[5] limited employment opportunities,[6] and a lessened probability of receiving life-saving emergency medical treatments.[7,8]

This book is about helping you become aware of your own unconscious biases, inspiring you to make a change, and then working to lock the new behavior in with a plan. This process model of change is the driving force behind my own research and will help you in your journey to be more inclusive.

Intro to a process model of change

When I first set out to write about unconscious bias, I had already researched and developed training for the 400+K IBM employees around the world and conducted hundreds of workshops, webinars, and talks on the subject. Based on this experience, I theorized that weakening unconscious bias was a process—it involved a change. This set me on the path of finding a model of change that would help me create a training. I wanted to find a solution that worked and went beyond just checking the diversity box.

I settled on the Lewin Model of Change—a three-step model of unfreeze, change, and refreeze. Step one involves destabilizing or unfreezing the current behavior before a new one can be adopted.[9] Step two focuses on moving or changing behavior. The last step of the model is refreezing and bringing in a new steady state to ensure there is no regression.[10] The Lewin Model of Change is well-accepted in management studies, and the flexibility of the model allowed me to take an active role in the process.

Wanting to do more than bring awareness or just share knowledge, I realized I needed a strong element of change in the middle part of the training. I wanted participants to walk away with a good sense of how to manage their unconscious biases, make change, and lock that change in. The experience needed to transcend the time spent with me in training to really penetrate the inner core of the person, so they would strive to overcome their unconscious biases after they left the confines of the classroom environment.

I knew from my own workshops that the portion of the training where participants paired up to share their experiences of how unconscious bias had affected their own lives was a critical turning point. This sharing is where the "aha" happened. These were the moments where the participants began to shift their perspectives and tried to understand the perspective of their partner. This is where empathy kicked in and change happened. I have named this element "transformational conversation."

Intro to transformational conversation

Transformational conversation is a conversation between people where each person shares their unique perspective and experience.[11] Transformational conversation occurs when people momentarily put aside their own perspective and start to really listen to the words being spoken in a conversation. They begin to imagine the world from their conversation partner's viewpoint as it described to them, and they transform or change.

Although transformational conversation is the key to change, it does not stand alone—thus why I emphasize a process model of change with transformational conversation at the core. The process model allows the person to come along the path of weakening unconscious bias in a formalized manner—from unfreezing the unconscious bias through awareness to changing through transformational conversation to refreezing the new behavior.

What to expect from this book

The goal of this book is to go beyond just educating you on unconscious bias. I want to change the way you think about unconscious bias and move you to change your own behavior. This book is a good start for your journey. And I call it a journey because you will have to be vigilant in your pursuit to diminish and overcome your unconscious biases. You have built up these biases over your lifetime, so this book is not an overnight fix.

As I mentioned earlier, this book follows the process model of change: unfreeze, change, and refreeze. We will first focus on unfreezing our current behavior and bringing awareness to the fact that we all have unconscious biases, just because we are human. You will learn about some of the research behind unconscious bias and about some common cognitive biases that impact our decision making. I will offer some examples that show how unconscious biases appear in an everyday context and why it is important to work to overcome our unconscious biases.

We will then focus on change and how we achieve that. We will talk about why traditional diversity training does not work and what does work. I will also dig deeper into transformational conversation and give you the tools to help you have these powerful conversations. This will bring us to how we create an environment of inclusion and allow diversity to flourish.

The last piece is to create a plan—refreezing the desirable behavior. We will talk about some of the elephants in the room when it comes to unconscious bias, diversity, and inclusion. This is important because we need to address how we plan to react and behave when we are confronted with those elephants and what we do when conversation does not work. When you finish this part and this book, you will be able to create your own plan for change and begin your journey with confidence.

I hope you will use this book as a catalyst for change. I hope you will come back to it as a reference and reread the parts that will help you in your everyday decision making. In addition, I hope that you will walk away as an advocate for change and share what you learn about unconscious bias.

But most of all, I hope that you will seek out individuals who you feel are different from you and have transformational conversations.

Chapter takeaways

- Every second, we are exposed to eleven million bits of data. Our brain can only consciously process around forty. Knowing this, it is easy to understand that everyone around us is experiencing a different reality.

- Unconscious bias is a bias (preference, inclination, prejudice) hidden from our conscious awareness. These biases are influenced by a lifetime of experiences, learnings, and interactions. And they affect how we react and behave.

- Our brain loves to categorize, allowing us to take the unknown and make it familiar.

- This book is based on a change model applied to unconscious bias: unfreeze the current, undesired behavior; change the behavior; and refreeze the new, desired behavior.

- Transformational conversation is part of this model of change. It is a conversation between people where each person shares their unique perspective and experience. The transformation comes when the listeners put aside their own perspective to really listen and engage with the speaker.

CHAPTER 2.

RECOGNIZE YOUR OWN BIASES.

Goal: Show that everyone has unconscious bias, through research, examples, and self-checks.

I was flying with my then three-year-old son for a clinical trial. At the airport, I was approached by a stranger. The woman looked at my son, who was chewing on a pacifier at the time and then looked up at me and asked, "Are you a special needs mom?" Cole was newly diagnosed with Hunter syndrome, so I wasn't really used to that title yet, but I nodded, thinking warily about where this conversation was going. She continued, "I'm a retired nurse. You special needs moms, I wouldn't trade places with you for anything in the world."

I was too shocked to reply. I couldn't believe this woman had gone out of her way to insult me and my child. She didn't know what our life was like. She was making assumptions. Perhaps in her mind, she was being compassionate? I don't know. But I do know that her unconscious bias allowed her to categorize me, "other" me, and to elevate herself above me in her mind.

How unconscious bias works

Mahzarin Banaji and Anthony Greenwald give this explanation of unconscious bias in their book *Blind Spot*: "What are hidden biases . . . bits of knowledge stored in our brains because we encounter them so frequently in our cultural environments. Hidden biases can influence our behavior toward members of particular social groups, but we remain oblivious to their influence."[1] When I share this definition in workshops, I always ask the participants if they would like to remain oblivious. Of course, they answer that they don't. And I will assume, reader, that you do not, as well, or you wouldn't have picked up this book.

If you were to search right now on the Internet for unconscious biases, you would come across at least 188 different ones. Many of the references would be to "cognitive biases," which are simply biases of the brain.[2]

These cognitive biases fall roughly into four categories:

1. **What should we remember?** Your brain is actively sorting through all the data you are receiving, trying to coalesce the information into a memory. We continue to edit and reinforce some memories after the fact. We discard specifics to form generalities. And we reduce events and lists to their key elements. Memories are stored differently based on how they were experienced.

2. **Too much information.** Too often we are bombarded with so much information that our brain can't possibly consciously pay attention to it all. Think of all the different sources of information, all those eleven million bits of data flooding into our brains. We need a way to manage that, so our brain makes decisions about what is kept, what is filed away, and what is discarded.

3. **Need to act fast.** There is a constant pull to make meaning of all the information pouring into our brains and to do so quickly, so often we go with the safe bet. We go with what we know, what is right in front of us. Think about all the times during the day when you react without really having the ability to slow down and reason through your decisions.

4. **Not enough meaning.** Then there is the part when we cannot gather enough meaning from what we know, so we search for the familiar. We seek to fill the vacuum of information. Our brains long for a cohesive story, so we fill in the blanks. We fill in characteristics and

actions for what we don't know. We even believe we know what someone is thinking.

As we try to make sense of a complex world, our cognitive biases try to help us. Sometimes that works well, but other times it can cause difficulties for us or those around us. With over 188 different cognitive biases, we won't go through them all in this book, but we will talk about the ones I see most often in the workplace. So, let's look at some examples of specific cognitive biases and how we can mitigate them.

Examples of bias

Confirmation bias

Suppose I say to you, "This beach only has pink shells on it." And then I proceed to walk down the beach only picking up the pinks shells and putting them in my bucket. I overlook the other colored shells and pay no attention to the sea glass or sand dollars on the beach. Then I come back to you and show you the contents of my bucket, "See, there are only pink shells." This is a simple example of confirmation bias. I am only picking up shells that confirm my statement that the beach only has pink shells. I am disregarding anything that contradicts my assertion. In this example, I may be making a conscious choice to only pick up pink shells to prove my point. Or I may unconsciously only see pink shells because that is what I am looking for.

Confirmation bias is driving us to seek out reinforcement or further evidence to prove our own viewpoint. We tend to search for, interpret, favor, and recall information in a way that confirms our own preexisting beliefs or hypotheses and give disproportionately less consideration to alternative possibilities. We do this all day as we decide what data we will consciously process and what data we will leave behind or file away.

Self-check

Think about the conversations you have and the news you watch. Do you only watch or listen to news programs that agree with your own beliefs? Are you already making your mind up and then mostly talking with people who have similar viewpoints and reinforce your own stance?

What do you do?

You have to slow down and call in your System 2. By slowing down, you can question your System 1 instincts and begin to create a fuller picture and viewpoint. You can ask others for their opinions. Get your news from a trustworthy source—even multiple sources. Broaden your circle of information with a diverse group of friends. Seek out alternative explanations, solutions, or results. The main point is to look outside of your own interests to see more than the pink shells on the beach.

Ingroup/Outgroup bias

"You know that Janet? She is new here. She came from marketing, so she really doesn't understand what we in communications are trying to accomplish."

"You salespeople are always overpromising to the client. You have no idea how we in development do our jobs."

"He is from the North, so he doesn't understand that we in the South move a little slower and politely wait until we are asked for our input."

In all these examples, the people are categorizing—breaking into groups of "Us" and "Them." Just like my story at the beginning of this chapter, each person is trying to distinguish themself from the "other." "We are the ingroup, and they are in the outgroup."

Unfortunately, this categorization usually leads us to behave more favorably toward people who are like us and unfavorably toward those we perceive as different. As I said in the beginning of the book, humans are constantly trying to make sense of the world around them. One way they do this is by putting people in familiar boxes—breaking them down into stereotypes they are comfortable with or have seen before. For example, millennials vs. boomers; citizens vs. immigrants; Democrats vs. Republicans; or Manchester United fan vs. Liverpool fan.

This last example comes from research done by Mark Levine.[3] He and some colleagues pulled together some Manchester United football fans and had them write an essay and fill out a questionnaire about their team. The researchers then told the fans they will watch a video on football in a nearby building and sent them in that direction. On their walk, they encountered a person who falls and cries out in pain from an injured ankle.

When the injured person is wearing a Manchester United jersey, 75 percent of the fans help the person. When the injured person is dressed in the jersey of rival team, Liverpool, or a generic sports jersey, only 35 percent of the fans help the person.

In a twist on the first experiment, the researchers changed the conditions by asking the football fans to respond to a questionnaire that emphasized their "overall love of the game." In this part of the study, 80 percent helped the injured person wearing the Manchester United jersey, but they also helped 70 percent of the time when the injured person was wearing a Liverpool jersey. The fans only helped 22 percent of the time when the injured person was dressed in a non-football sports jersey.

So, what can we learn from this experiment? We can see that ingroup/outgroup ties can influence our behavior. When we consider ourselves part of the same group, we are more likely to engage. When we consider the other person as outside our group, we are less likely to engage.

Self-check

Do you tend to make statements separating yourself from others in attempt to show your group as superior? Do you try to garner favor from someone else by showing you are in their "ingroup"? Are you creating divisions of "Us" and "Them"?

What do you do?

Examine why you are leaving someone out. Is your position being threatened? Could you benefit from an outside perspective? Listen to conversations carefully for traces of "us and them" influences, and refocus the discussion with inclusive language and behavior. We will learn more about how to do this in a later chapter.

Similarity bias and affinity bias

My first job out of college was working for a non-profit in Knoxville, Tennessee. I was new to fundraising, so I had a lot to learn. Luckily, the director of the organization was willing to teach me. She was from New York, so she was an unlikely match for the East Tennessee area. She usually tried to mask her accent because folks in this part of the country tended to be distrustful of outsiders asking for money. We both soon saw this in action when we went to pitch a fifty-thousand-dollar sponsorship to the major country radio station in our area. Before we went in, the director said she would handle the presentation, so I should just watch to see how it was done. But as soon as we sat down with the general manager, he looked straight at me and said he knew me from somewhere. We talked for a while about where we could have met or mutual friends we may have, but we didn't figure out our commonality. However, during that time, the director slid the proposal over to me and said, "Kim is going to give you more information about how you can help our organization." My business-savvy director intended for me to take full advantage of my perceived similarity with the general manager to secure the sponsorship. For the record, I did.

Similarity bias is our tendency to behave more favorably toward someone we perceive as like us. With affinity bias, we behave more favorably when we perceive we have an affinity or commonality between us. I group them together because we often see them occurring together. We are actively seeking out people we are like, so we feel comfortable. We know what to expect from them. And in this pursuit, we look for things we have in common, and we see these seeming similarities or affinities as proxies for trust and attention.

Every time I talk about similarity bias in a workshop, I struggle with the perceived benefit versus the drawback. Almost everyone at some point in their lives has benefited from similarity bias or affinity bias—me included. My Southern accent tends to be stronger when I am conducting a workshop in the South versus when I try to mask it when I am in the North, Mideast, or Midwest. I am unconsciously trying to make myself more like my audience.

The superintendent of a utility company heard me speak on unconscious bias at a local HR event. He came up to me afterward: "I could argue with you all day about how my biases have served me well in my life. But I would like you to come talk to my employees. I don't know exactly what we need at my company. I just know my employees are so set in their ways, and I think you can help." I was not surprised by the first comment. I had heard it before, but I was intrigued by the second part and eager to find out how I could apply what I knew to the utility industry.

After meeting with the superintendent to find out what specific issues he wanted addressed, I set out to create the curriculum for our upcoming workshop. I would have seven managers—six men and one woman. I remember the day I delivered the training, I watched closely as each participant walked into the room. I felt my own unconscious biases running wild. The first two people who arrived were older, white males with skeptical faces who seemed wary of this "diversity lady" coming in to teach them—friendly but reserved. The next two were white males close to middle age, and they seemed unsure of what to expect. I was pleased to see a receptive face with the woman. Of course, I knew I had the support of the superintendent, so this gave me some confidence. Still, when the last man came in, I was temporarily doubtful of how my approach to unconscious bias training would play out. He was a white man in his early sixties. He wore jeans, work boots, a t-shirt, and a chain securely holding his wallet in his pocket. A cap covered his salt-and-pepper hair and big-rimmed glasses hid his eyes, and I caught a glimpse of skepticism behind his long gray beard. I felt like he was going to be the toughest one in the audience. Again, I was being influenced by my own biases—making assumptions based on his appearance.

As we were each sizing each other up, I told them that my grandparents and my mom grew up just down the road from where we were now—in Madisonville and Ballplay. I saw some astonished faces, but then a quick change to relaxation. I was one of them. Surely, I would not come there to shame them if I had the same "upbringing" that they did? Similarity bias helped me here because it allowed me to be considered as part of the ingroup. I was no longer an outsider. So, they could relax a bit and let down their guard.

As it turned out, the eight of us had a great session. I opened with my usual introduction on awareness, but with a focus on the cognitive biases that we all have. This immediately seemed to put the group at ease. I was not there to attack, judge, or finger point. In this instance, similarity bias had served me well. But I was very deliberate with this one. It wasn't something I was doing unconsciously.

By slowing down to check yourself, as I did, you can understand whether you are harming someone else with your unconscious biases.

Self-check

Do you find yourself looking for similarities between yourself and others? Are you comparing the person to the present you or a younger you? For example, "You remind me of myself when I first started out in my career." Have you said, "I just don't get a good vibe from them?" "Or I'm going to go with my gut on this one." These could also be signs that your biases are playing a role in your decision making.

In your personal life, think about the people in your immediate friend circle. Have you surrounded yourself with people who are just like you? Do you have friends or colleagues who have different ideas, backgrounds, experiences than you? How diverse are they?

What do you do?

Pick the right person for the team, not the person who looks best on paper or the person you have the most in common with. You are looking for a fit for a job role, not a replica of yourself. If you find you have recruited, hired, or promoted someone who is a "good fit," look closely at your own biases.

If you find yourself allowing similarity bias or affinity bias to impact your decision making, write down what you like about that person. Compare that to yourself. Is it the same or different? Ask, "Do I need someone just like me on the team?" You don't need five people on a team that have the same ideas, opinions, and background. You only need one of them.

Halo/Horn effect

"Shantell is such a great student, but she didn't turn in this last assignment. Something must be wrong. I should check in with her to see how I can help."

"Jackson didn't turn in this last assignment. But that is not surprising. He always comes to class late. I don't think he really cares about this class at all."

These examples are typical halo/horn effect behavior. In the case of Shantell, she has been given a halo. She is deemed good, and everything she touches or does must also be good. If she fails in some aspect, we will consider this an anomaly and dismiss it. For Jackson, we have deemed him bad and given him horns. Everything he does is overshadowed by the idea that he is not good, so his negative actions are considered the norm and expected. If he does anything good, we will chalk that up to be a fluke or ignore it entirely.

We can think of the halo/horn effect as our tendency to base our perceptions of a person on a single, positive trait (halo) or negative trait (horn). This could be a physical trait, something about the person's history, like where they attended college, or a perception about a particular group of people.

Self-check

Have you ever found yourself trying to turn a positive about a person into a negative, just because you do not like that person? Have you dismissed someone outright and not listened to his/her ideas because you have deemed that person bad? Have you done the opposite and approved of someone's idea just because you like them or because you think everything they do is good? Have you ever used the words, "Those people" in a sentence, like "Those people from Harvard . . ."? Or "Those people who don't speak plain English . . ."? These generalities can be a sign of the halo/horn effect.

What can you do?

If you are accessing a person for a job role or promotion, write out the positive and negative traits of the person. Work to see everyone as an individual and make decisions based on experiences with that person alone. Ask for other opinions about the person and try to really listen without judgment—hear without trying to come up with your own rebuttal or agreement. We will talk more about how to listen well later in the book.

Bandwagon bias and group think

The meeting had just concluded. Jan and Mark were walking back to their offices when Jan said, "You know, that plan we talked about in the meeting is not going to work."

"What do you mean? Everyone agreed to it," said Mark.

"Well, I have doubts. I don't think we really thought about the customer's viewpoint," said Jan.

"Why didn't you say something in the meeting?" Mark replied.

"Well, everyone else seemed to be backing our manager's plan, so I didn't want to ruffle any feathers," said Jan.

Not wanting to go against the group is exactly what is behind bandwagon bias. With bandwagon bias, we tend to go along with something because we think other people are doing it, regardless of our own beliefs. As Jan said, we may not want to "ruffle any feathers" or disagree with an authority figure or the majority.

Unfortunately, this behavior can lead to erroneous decision making. If you or someone else just goes along with the crowd when you think differently, you are limiting the knowledge of the group. You are leading to a culture of groupthink, which is a similar bias.

Groupthink happens when we are trying to minimize conflict by converging on a decision that appears to be gathering support. Again, we will see people not speaking up because they feel like their opinion doesn't matter or won't be heard. With groupthink, people begin to either buy-in to the group argument, or with bandwagon bias, they tend to join the crowd because it seems the majority is trending toward a certain direction. Both biases have the impact of silencing the minority opinion. And in many cases, they may silence those that also agree with the minority opinion.

Self-check

Have you ever sat in a meeting thinking, "Well, it seems everyone has already made up their minds, so I will just go along" or "It really doesn't matter what I say, so I will just go with rest of the group"? These are thoughts that lead to bandwagon bias and groupthink.

What can you do?

Share your opinions, even if they are contrary to the group's. Others may be waiting for someone else to speak up. Also, ask for conflicting opinions or dissenting views. When you see someone staying quiet, ask what they think.

Play devil's advocate or if you are the leader in a meeting, ask someone else to play devil's advocate and adopt the opposite position.

Groupthink and bandwagon bias discourage individual responsibility and creativity, which is the next bias we will discuss.

Creativity bias

Not too long ago, I was piloting a program on unconscious bias with a client. They had asked me to work with them because they needed some help in shifting the culture. I began by talking about unconscious bias awareness and change. As I started diving into the cognitive biases that hold companies back from innovating, specifically creativity bias, the grumbling began:

"We can't talk about creativity bias here. There's no way that will fly here—that's not our culture." "We can't talk to employees about creativity bias because they will get frustrated when they are not able to be innovative." And believe it or not, "It's just not going to work here. We have a very unique culture—not open to outside thinking."

I was shocked to find the very ones who would be leading the company were illustrating creativity bias themselves.

During my career in the corporate world, I recall many times being told I could not implement a creative solution because that's "not the way we do things around here." Or "you will never get that past legal." It's understandable in a way. Large companies have more to lose, so they stick with what is safe—what is proven and certain. And we as individuals are comfortable with the familiar.

Creativity requires trying something never done before, moving away from the known to the unknown, and ultimately risking failure. It is easy to say we want our employees to be creative, but it's a very different thing to give them the freedom to make changes. For many of us, we have a creativity bias like the company in my example. We tend to shy away from anything that is different than the status quo because of the fear of uncertainty.

Take this well-cited example of Kodak:

Kodak engineer Steve Sasson patented the digital photography technology in 1978. When he presented it to the corporate executives, they could not imagine a world without film. And they did not want to—they were making money every step of the way in the film process. As you probably know, Kodak filed for bankruptcy in 2012. Because they did not accept change and embrace creativity, they were left behind.[4]

Companies need to allow for failure—fail, but fail fast. Cognitively, we know of the innovation that has come from failures—the light bulb, the sticky note, the telephone, etc. And we tell employees to think creatively, be innovative, but what we really mean is "within these parameters—you get it right the first time, you don't spend any money, and you don't deviate from what we are comfortable with."

Self-check

Have you ever said to anyone, "That's not the way we do things around here?" Or have you shut someone down before they shared their complete idea because "it will never work here"? Are you really listening when people share an idea that is different from your own, or are you mentally thinking about your argument against their idea?

What can you do?

Risk intolerance has consequences. By not embracing creativity or the next innovation, you are essentially condemning yourself to stagnation. So how do you mitigate creativity bias?

1. **Be okay with uncertainty.** If you are trying something new, you will not know all the outcomes. For those that need a small step before the big leap: Try a pilot. Test out the solution, program, etc. with a small group before taking it to the entire company.

2. **Do a pre-mortem.** Gather people you trust with diverse viewpoints, and work through a pre-mortem to talk through what could go wrong, but also what could go right.

3. **Allow creative people some freedom, time, and space to innovate.** Creative ideas don't always pop up overnight or even at the office. Creatives need the flexibility to think and play. Imposing strict rules and parameters will impede "thinking outside the box."

4. **Encourage collaboration.** Diversity bonuses come from teaming up people with different perspectives—the perfect environment for creativity to thrive.

5. **Trust your employees and give them the tools and resources to push the boundaries.** Back off from micro-managing, constant updates, and pointless interference. In other words, don't get in the way of creative ideas.

6. **Allow for failure.** Some creative ideas are not going to work out. But don't allow your own biases to hold others back from trying.

The bottom line is that you cannot have creativity without change. With change comes some risk, but it also has great rewards.

Why does unconscious bias matter?

As we have seen from the previous examples in this chapter, knowing how unconscious bias influences us is important because it impacts real-world decisions. And lack of awareness can lead to unintentional behavior.[5,6,7] This process leads people to be unwittingly complicit in the perpetuation of discrimination.[8] "Data on implicit or unconscious bias are surprising and even troubling because individuals and even professionals, whose conscious values reveal no intent to harm, nevertheless show systematic and selective patterns of decision-making that result in differential treatment."[9]

We will examine this "differential treatment" in the next chapter and look at some specific examples of how bias in the workplace can lead to unintended or adverse consequences.

Chapter takeaways

- Cognitive biases fall roughly into four categories: (1) What should you remember, (2) Too much information, (3) Need to act fast, and (4) Not enough meaning.

- Confirmation bias drives us to seek out only information that reinforces our own viewpoint.

- With ingroup/outgroup bias, we categorize everyone around us into those we accept (good) and those we do not (bad).

- Similarity bias leads us to seek out those who are like us. Affinity bias leads us to associate with people who we have something in common with.

- With the halo/horn effect, we tend to disregard detail, and paint everything someone does as either good (halo) or bad (horn).

- Bandwagon bias happens when we go along with a group and disregard anything that contradicts the group opinion. Groupthink is similar because it shuts down any ideas that fall outside the perceived popular opinion.

- Creativity bias is a bias against creativity. It is an aversion to creativity when there is a possibility of risk or failure.

CHAPTER 3.

SEE THE BIAS AROUND YOU.

Goal: Illustrate how unconscious bias impacts our decision-making and our everyday interactions.

"I was working as a sales rep in South Chicago. I was working with mostly white males. My boss was a white male, and my counterpart for another region was a white male. I did well, and my numbers were consistently high. My male colleague was not doing so well.

So, my boss called a meeting with the two of us. He turned to my male colleague and asked him as he gestured in my direction, 'Why aren't your numbers as good as hers?'

I was surprised. Why didn't he ask me why my numbers were so high? Why didn't he ask me the reason behind my success? Why did he assume that there was something my male colleague wasn't doing well as opposed to something I was doing that was extraordinary?"

This is example of the white male being depicted as the norm—the dominant social identity. The white male colleague is the starting point, the standard. If the Black female is doing better than the male, the white male must be performing below the norm. The possibility of the Black female performing above the "norm" does not enter the boss's thinking, in this case. This is unconscious bias at work. This is a person's social identity (Black female) being evaluated against the standard social identity—that of a White male.

Also, in this example, the woman is experiencing multiple biases directed toward her, both racial bias and gender bias. In this case, they overlap. It's hard to tell if she is being discriminated against because she is Black or because she is a woman. Likely, it's a bit of both. This is what we call intersectionality, and the bias is multiplied.

Bias in the workplace

I often hold unconscious bias workshops with human resource (HR) professionals. After all, they are on the frontline of most recruiting, hiring, development, and promotion decisions. And this also gives them an opportunity to have a substantial impact on the makeup of the employee population and the culture of the company. This can be seen as both a good and a bad thing.

I ask the participants to share what bothers them when they are interviewing—what will make them consider not hiring an employee. I am amazed at their answers: chipped nail polish, visible tattoos, too many piercings, overly nervous and sweating, wrinkled shirt, too much makeup, too little makeup, too much perfume, long beards, and more. These are all external factors that would have nothing to do with how someone would perform in their job, yet these HR professionals are allowing them to influence their decision making.

I also ask how many people are using structured interview questions. Again, I am amazed when only a few hands go up. Of course, the obvious next question is, "How do you conduct your interviews?" Here is a smattering of the answers: "I just talk to the person to get an idea of who they are and if they will fit into our company culture." And "I ask the person to tell me about themselves and why they want the job." Or my personal favorite, "I usually go with my gut. I can tell in the first few minutes whether or not I will hire the person."

I hope you see in those answers all the potential for bias and start to recognize many of the cognitive biases we discussed in the last chapter. You are basically surrendering your recruiting, hiring, and promotion decisions to your previous assumptions, prejudices, and biases. You may think you are being objective, but a process without structure is almost entirely subjective. Artificial intelligence (AI) gives some options, but perhaps you are not quite ready to hand over the reins to algorithms. So, how do we start to eliminate some of the biases in ourselves?

Hiring and promotion decisions

Let's look again at some of the cognitive biases we talked about in the last chapter in the workplace context.

Overconfidence bias – the tendency people have to be more confident in their own abilities than is objectively reasonable.

Overconfidence bias comes into play in hiring when we think we are better at hiring than we are. The research says that there is a fifty percent failure rate for new hires, so this seems to be an area where we could all use a little help. If you are one of those that "goes with your gut" when hiring, you may be relying too much on your own biases.

Halo/Horn effect – the tendency to base your perception of a person on a single, positive trait (halo) or negative trait (horn).

It is obvious how the halo or horn effect could impact a hiring or promotion decision. You may decide an attractive person is more qualified for a job (halo effect) or an unattractive person in less qualified (horn effect). You have essentially taken one trait of the person and associated it with a totally unrelated area, such as competency, honesty, and reliability.

Confirmation bias – the tendency to search for, interpret, favor, and recall information that confirms your preexisting beliefs, while discarding or discounting anything that does not.

Confirmation bias builds upon all the other biases. If we make an opinion about a person within the first few minutes we meet them, we tend to only look at evidence that validates that opinion. For example, you meet someone whose shirt is wrinkled and think that he obviously does not care about his appearance. Throughout the interview, you will zero in on any evidence that shows lack of attention to detail or disorganization.

Similarity bias – the tendency to favor people just like us.

We all know that we tend to like people who are similar to us. We are comfortable with them. We know what to expect. But do we really want an office full of people like ourselves? During one of my workshops, I remember an executive saying, "I want people who are different. Why would I want five people who all act and think the same way? I don't need five of them. I only need one." Keep this in mind when you feel you have a real "connection" with the person you are interviewing.

Gender and racial bias – the tendency to overlook the nuances and individual characteristics of a person and rely on generalities and stereotypes.

Both gender and racial bias can fit into all the examples. Again, we tend to favor people who are like us, and often in the workplace, White males are in the power position of hiring and promoting. Let me share some specific examples of unconscious biases impacting women in the workplace.

One workshop participant described incidents where she would share her opinion and her manager would immediately turn to one of her male colleagues to validate what she said: "Do you agree with that? What do you think about what she said?" The subtlety is that the manager did not do this when his male employees stated an opinion. To the female employee, it was as if her own opinion was not valuable or even valid until a male colleague agreed. And sometimes this questioning by the manager would evolve into mansplaining—where her male colleague would say something like, "What I think she is trying to say is . . ." In which case, the manager would congratulate the male colleague on the idea that had just been expressed by the female employee. For the female employee, this was exasperating.

One woman spoke about a time she was negotiating a major sales deal. The other side was not budging much on their demands. When she reported to her management team about her progress, they asked her if she was being "aggressive enough." "What we need is someone to really come down hard on them and make them understand our position." When she explained that she had done all of that, her manager told her that he wanted to be in on future calls. The implication was clear—a female could not negotiate from a power position. She obviously did not know what she was doing.

Removing unconscious bias from the process

So, what do we do about unconscious bias?

1. *Slow down.* Be aware of your own biases. If you are rushing through the hiring process, you are not allowing time for your System 2 to kick in. And chances are you aren't really listening to the person you are talking to—you are making assumptions, comparing them to someone you have met before, and making judgments based on appearance.

2. *Reduce distractions.* When we try to complete several complex tasks at one time, we tend to fall back on automatic thinking, leaving us open to errors and biases. If you are talking to someone face-to-face, move away from your computer, turn off your phone, and really focus on the words the person is saying.

3. *Don't make assumptions.* Much of the time we are not looking at the totality of the person. We are generalizing about "someone like them." Make sure you are truly listening to what the other person is saying and not skipping to the part where you talk.

4. *Ask for other opinions and perspectives.* Most likely, others will focus on different aspects of a conversation or qualities in the applicant than you would. If you are holding a panel-type interview or have

multiple interviewers, make sure you have already rated the applicant before you have others weigh in. (See number 8 on structured
interview questions.)

If you are specifically focused on recruitment and hiring, think about
the following:

5. *Hire for the skills needed for the job.* List only the criteria necessary
   for the job. If the applicant does not need a master's degree for the
   job, don't put it as a requirement. You can say "Bachelor's degree
   required. Master's degree preferred."

6. *Use gender-neutral language in job ads and job descriptions.* This
   goes beyond using gender-neutral pronouns. The actual wording
   can influence who responds to your ad. Words like "guru, hack-
   ing, and competitive" can keep female applicants from applying.
   Women tend to look for words like "teaming, commitment, and
   sympathetic"—terms considered more feminine.[1]

7. *Blind your resume review process.* There are several computer programs and sites to help with this, but a sticky note works also. Cover
   up the name when you are reviewing resumes.

8. *Use structured interview questions.*[2] This is a big one. If you go into
   the interview unprepared, you are allowing more of your biases to
   lead you. Here's some guidance:

   • Think of six skills/traits the applicant needs for the job. (Example:
     technical, reliable, etc.)

   • Make a list of questions for each trait, and think about how you
     will score it (Example: 1–5). You should have a good idea of what
     is weak and what is strong.

   • Collect information on one trait at a time, scoring as you go
     before you move to the next question.

   • Add up the six scores. Pick the candidate with the highest score.

If you use this scoring system with multiple interviewers (seeking other opinions), make sure you each score separately and only compare scores at the end. Ensure you don't change your scoring at the end to fit the narrative you are creating about a person. If you want to fairly compare your candidates, you don't want to put your thumb on the scale for one over another.

Here's an example from a structured interview for a non-profit operations manager position:

Ratings: (*Rate as you go. Do not wait until the end*)

1 – Not good & don't see a way up.

2 – Would catch on, but needs coaching.

3 – Good Potential/Minimal coaching needed.

4 – Great—got this, no coaching needed.

Self-starter/works without constant supervision	Rating
1. Are you good at managing yourself?	4
2. What is your ideal work environment?	3
Organized	
3. How do you keep yourself organized when dealing with tasks & requests from multiple sources?	4
4. Do you have a quiet space and time to work uninterrupted?	3
Operations Experience (day-to-day)	
5. What do you think are the key personal strengths of a non-profit office manager?	3
6. What office manager duties do you enjoy most & least?	2
Communication Skills	
7. When you have a challenge or difficulty, how do you react?	2
8. Tell me about a situation where you have had to handle a difficult client?	2

Financially-minded	
9. What is your comfort level with handling the day-to-day finances for a 2M+ organization?	4
10. What is your experience in this area?	4
Dependable/Reliable	
11. How do you manage confidential information?	4
12. Tell me about a time you made a mistake at work and how you fixed it.	3
Total	**38**

Some will push back that a structured interview is too impersonal or sterile: "You don't really get a sense of the person." But I would say to them, "Aren't you trying to determine the skill level of the interviewee? Can you think of a skill or trait needed that will help you determine more about the person? And you can always ask follow-up questions, but structure ensures you are asking all the same questions of each interviewee and giving everyone a fair shot at the job.

Of course, one of the best ways to start eliminating your biases is through education. Learn more about cognitive biases, so you can make decisions based on reliable information, rather than your gut feeling. We will get further into dealing with unconscious bias in the next chapter when we talk about the process model of change and transformational conversation.

Chapter takeaways

- Cognitive biases can disrupt the hiring process. Make sure to use structured interviews to minimize the influence of bias.

- Some common biases to watch out for in hiring and promoting include the following: overconfidence bias, halo/horn effect, confirmation bias, similarity bias, gender bias, and racial bias.

- To reduce unconscious bias, do the following: (1) Slow down, (2) Reduce distractions, (3) Don't make assumptions, and (4) Ask for other opinions and perspectives.

- When recruiting and hiring for a job, follow this procedure: (1) Hire for the skills needed for the job, (2) Use gender neutral language in job ads and descriptions, (3) Blind your resume review process, and (4) Use structured interview questions.

CHAPTER 4.

TAKE STEPS TO MINIMIZE YOUR BIAS.

Goal: Introduce the audience to transformational conversation and process model of change.

A friend of mine and I were having a conversation when she said, "Well, we have to be careful. We don't want people going off the reservation."

I was quite taken aback, but I quickly said to her: "You can't say that."

She said, "Say what?" She had no clue she had said something offensive. When I pointed out that she had said, "off the reservation," she still didn't know what was wrong. I told her this was offensive because we were implying that someone "going off the reservation" is a reference to trying to keep Native Americans on the reservations or in their "place."

As soon as I gave my explanation, she said, "Oh, my gosh. I never even thought of that." That was the response I had expected. Most of us don't think carefully about the origins of things we say every day. We have heard them our whole lives, and we just repeat them.

As Maya Angelou said, "Do the best you can until you know better. Then when you know better, do better."[1]

Here's another example. I'm from Tennessee, so I'm a huge Dolly Parton fan. And she reinforced my reverence for her in a 2020 interview with Billboard Magazine talking about renaming her Dixie Stamped attraction to The Stampede in 2018:

> There's such a thing as innocent ignorance, and so many of us are guilty of that. When they said "Dixie" was an offensive word, I thought, Well, I don't want to offend anybody. This is a business. We'll just call it "The Stampede." As soon as you realize that [something] is a problem, you should fix it. Don't be a dumbass. That's where my heart is. I would never dream of hurting anybody on purpose.[2]

Just as we don't want to be oblivious to our biases, I hope we also don't want to be "dumbasses."

Making a change

When I first started researching what works in making a change in unconscious bias, I was discouraged. There didn't seem to be a proven formula. However, there has been substantial research on unconscious bias, so I dug in and broadened my research.

I knew from my previous work on unconscious bias that the point in the workshop where participants talked with each other about a time unconscious bias impacted them was a special moment and a turning point. But I did not at that time have the "why" fully fleshed out. I found my "why" in the work of Patricia Devine on breaking the prejudice habit, and her research led me to Gordon Allport's groundbreaking work on contact theory. Extensive research has shown that contact results in a reduction in prejudice, so I reasoned that it could also be successful with unconscious bias.[3,4]

Based on Contact Theory, I theorized that a specific part of contact—what I call transformational conversation—would lead to change in unconscious bias. The Cambridge Dictionary defines conversation as "an informal, usually private talk in which two or more people exchange thoughts, feelings, or ideas."[5] However, transformational conversation is a specific type of conversation—conversation between two or more people who share their own perspective that results in a transformation of thought.

Conversation as a method of change is backed by the research into empathy and perspective shifts. Baron-Cohen describes empathy this way: "Empathy helps you tune in to someone else's world; you have to set aside your own world—your perception, knowledge, assumptions, or feelings."[6] During the transformational conversation piece of the workshop, participants employ empathy to shift their perspective. Research has shown that a perspective shift is needed for behavioral change, so conversation is a critical piece to changing unconscious bias.

So, now I had a theory (contact theory) and research (reducing prejudice) to guide my hypothesis, I needed a model of change.

Process model of change

Behavior change is the holy grail of workshop training. And I set my expectations high. I chose the Lewin Model of Change because it is well-established in the research literature as an effective model, and the seemingly simplistic nature of the three-step model—unfreeze, change, refreeze—lent itself well to a workshop focused on unconscious bias.[7]

I adapted Lewin's model slightly to create a process model of change for implicit bias/unconscious bias. I will break down each step, so you can either recreate the process or use it to judge the effectiveness of the training in this area.

Figure 1: Process Model of Change for Implicit Bias

Unfreeze

To motivate someone to unfreeze a current behavior, you first have to make them aware of what that behavior is. Social psychology research has shown that people are often unaware of their own biases, so they first need to acknowledge them before they can begin to hold themselves accountable.[8,9]

As described in Chapter 2, I focus first on the cognitive biases that we all have because we are humans. My goal is behavior change, so I can best achieve that by avoiding threat[10], shaming[11,12], and divisive rhetoric.[13] These approaches can doom unconscious bias training from the start. I also don't make assumptions about the participants' unconscious biases based on historical prejudice or assumed intentional bias.[14,15,16,17] Research shows these do not work.

Starting with cognitive biases, such as affinity bias or similarity bias, is a more subtle and effective way of raising awareness and can make the difference on whether the message is heard, ignored, or resented. Everyone immediately recognizes these biases in themselves, so they are more open to the need for change. Race and gender will inevitably come up in the discussion, but not in a finger-pointing context. And the added benefit of cognitive bias training is that you are giving people tools to apply to any situation—whether interacting with a person of a different race, gender, or religion to someone who is LGBTQ+ or has a disability.

Once general awareness about unconscious bias is established, you can then take participants through exercises where they can begin to uncover their own biases—exercises showing errors in thinking, assumptions, and associations.

Change

The middle piece of the process model contains the key element of change—transformational conversation, so I will spend more time describing it. This is the point in the workshop where I break up the participants into groups for conversation. But before I do that, I give them two tools to help them analyze their unconscious biases: Chris Argyris' *The Ladder of Influence*[18] and a mental model—Bias Feedback Loop, based on the Patricia Devine's research on "breaking" prejudice.[19,20]

The ladder of inference

The Ladder of Inference can be used to help a person work through their unconscious biases. It forces the person to slow down to think through the steps of a decision or action. Here's how it works, starting from the bottom of the ladder.

1. Out of the eleven-million bits of data available to us at any one time, we make a selection;

2. From that selection, we begin to draw meaning;

3. That meaning leads to assumptions;

4. Those assumptions lead us to a conclusion;

5. We adapt our beliefs; and

6. We take action.

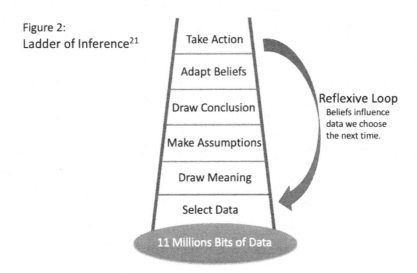

Figure 2:
Ladder of Inference[21]

This is a reflexive loop, so the previous cycle can determine what data we select the next time and our next set of actions. But what happens if we make a mistake anywhere along the ladder? The obvious answer is it affects the next step you take. Let's look at an example.

I was working from my home office, and my boss was at an onsite location of the company in another state. We were talking over the phone during our weekly meeting, and I excitedly began detailing a plan I had for revolutionizing our diversity strategy. As I spoke, I heard her typing. I thought: "She is working on something else and not listening to me. She doesn't respect my creativity or opinions. She never gives me credit for my ideas. I need to find a new job."

After a few moments, she stopped typing and said to me, "Kim, this is a great idea. I'm just taking notes, so I get the details right when I run this by the senior executives."

So, where did I go wrong? She was typing, so the data I pulled was correct. But the meaning I was giving the typing was wrong. I attributed it to her being distracted and not listening to me. From there I ran wild with my assumptions and was ready to quit my job—all over a bad assumption.

From this example, you can see how quickly I moved up the ladder in a matter of seconds. So, it's important to slow down to allow yourself to go through each step of the ladder, carefully accessing each rung.

Here's an example from one of my workshops. After the participants broke up into groups for their transformational conversations, I brought them back together to discuss any insights that came from their conversation. I asked if anyone wanted to share their experience. A tall, husky, older gentleman volunteered. I will call him Jack.

> I remember I was stuck in construction traffic one afternoon. We were barely moving. I was getting frustrated. As I finally got up to the intersection, a cop let a man in a car pull out in front of me. This made me angry. Here I was waiting my turn in this long line, and this guy just pulls out in front of me. I was mad. As the traffic started moving, I followed this guy down to the next light. I got out of my car, walked up to his window, and angrily tapped on his window. He rolled down his window, and I saw he was an elderly gentleman. I felt terrible.

I probed a bit into this situation, trying to help Jack understand his own reactions. Why did he feel terrible?

Jack said he felt terrible because he had acted on his assumptions. He has assumed that this guy was a jerk and intended to cut line. He had not considered the man's perspective. I asked him to take us through the situation using the Ladder of Inference.

- What data did you choose? "I chose that this guy pulled out in front of me."

- What assumption did you make from that? "The guy was a jerk."

- What conclusion did you come to? "The guy was trying to cheat and get ahead of me." How did you alter your beliefs? "I thought that everyone is trying to take advantage of me."

- What action did you take? "I chased him down."

After going through this exercise in front of the group, I asked them where Jack had fallen off the ladder. The data he selected was valid—the guy did pull out in front of him. But as Jack himself pointed out, he had made the wrong assumption. The guy wasn't a jerk. He was an elderly man that needed a little help to navigate traffic. Unfortunately, Jack had already jumped up the ladder and was chasing the guy down for his wrong assumption. This was sobering to Jack and the other participants. They could all relate to this example of intolerance. They too had instances of times when anger and frustration led them down the wrong path.

Bias feedback loop

The Bias Feedback Loop is another tool to help you slow down. It is based upon the idea that people need feedback that contradicts their assumptions to break the cycle of reinforcing biases.[22,23]

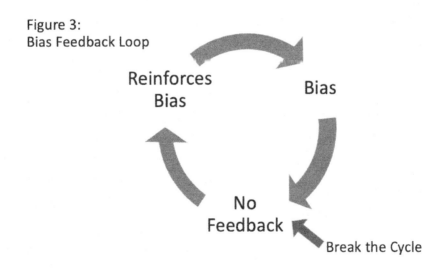

Figure 3:
Bias Feedback Loop

Reinforces
Bias

Bias

No
Feedback

Break the Cycle

The cycle works like this:

- A person encounters a situation that triggers an assumption based on a previous experience or stereotype.

- From there, they can choose one of two paths: (a) seek feedback on that assumption (bias), or (b) don't seek feedback on that assumption.

- If the person does not seek feedback or more information, they are essentially reinforcing that bias and giving it more weight. If the person does seek feedback, they add more information to the assumption, which may or may not contradict the bias.

- Each time the person cycles through the loop, they are reinforcing the bias, stereotype, or prejudice, depending on the content of the assumption.

For example, Elizabeth had a belief that all sorority girls were snobbish and superficial. She had met a few ladies who fit that description, so her bias was reinforced. However, one day when she was visiting my apartment and saw some of my sorority pictures, she looked at the pictures, and I heard her say, "Huh!?"

She liked me, and I didn't fit her model of being snobbish or superficial. Elizabeth now had new feedback to interrupt her bias feedback loop. As a result, she was questioning her bias.

I ask participants to use the feedback loop to seek out more information when they find themselves making assumptions, stereotyping, or triggering biases.

Both tools encourage a conversation with ourselves—questioning our assumptions and taking steps to right our path. It's like having an imaginary referee calling a timeout for your brain to reprocess information more slowly—a replay, if you will.

Transformational conversation

Okay, now we will get back to transformational conversations and change. Based on research from social psychologist Joy-Gaba, I begin with an experiential learning environment. I hold face-to-face classes and limit the size to less than twenty-five when possible. Participants should have ample opportunities to interact with each other, and I deliberately set up encounters for those with different social identities (based on gender and race in this case, but it could be any difference: religion, socioeconomic status, etc.) to have transformational conversations.

Specifically, I ask participants to break up in groups of two or three and discuss a situation where unconscious bias has played a role. I tell them they can share experiences where they are on the receiving end or the giving side. The other person is instructed to listen and not talk until the first speaker has finished. Then, together, they can discuss what they did well and what they could have done differently. Then, they switch roles. If time permits, each person can relate a story of both being on the receiving end and the giving side of unconscious bias.

Here are some examples of how these conversations went.

Case Study: George and Tracy

You may recall George's story of his own unconscious bias toward a Black male from Chapter 1. George was paired with Tracy, an African-American female from the US, and Kalil from Sudan.

> I'm out in the parking lot, and I'm walking in by myself, and there is um, there's uh, another young man coming in—Black guy, long dreadlocks, a big strong-looking guy, real young. And we're walking in and initially, you know, kind of like, you know, when you're walking, "Okay. There's a person. There is a person there. Okay, no big deal." And then he keeps looking at me, you know? So now it's like [making radar sound] "beep, beep . . ." [laughing] Why, why is he looking at me?
>
> And he walks over and says, "Hey, do I, do I know you?" and I'm looking at him like, "I don't think so." I slowed down, and then he stopped. So, I kept walking, and he said, "No, really, really, I know you." So, I stopped, and I was like, "I really don't think you do. I don't recognize you." Now I'm getting . . . I'm

getting scared. I, you know, my initial fight or flight thought was like starting to kick in . . .

When I spoke with Tracy after the workshop, she said she was not surprised by George's story: "I guess being an African-American, I guess I'm used to people having, you know, maybe that perception."

Tracy offered more insight about the conversation:

> It was nice that he felt comfortable enough to have that conversation with us, especially with me being there and maybe trying not to offend me but at the same time trying to explain his story . . . so that was nice because some people aren't brave enough to have that type of conversation with other people. I was even surprised in that sense that he felt comfortable enough to bring forth, out of all the examples in the world he could have picked potentially, you know, the thought was that he felt comfortable and safe enough in our group to bring that up and have a conversation without maybe possibly feeling judged by myself or by Kalil or the whole group.

Instead of being offended or upset, as might be expected, Tracy felt George was "brave." This revelation made even further sense when coupled with Tracy's final workshop reflection: "The conversations provided additional examples for deeper understanding." Tracy looked beyond George's racial bias to try to see his perspective. In her post-workshop interview, when speaking of her own plan for addressing unconscious bias, she said:

> . . .first, I should be more open-minded to the differences between people and how they may look at things differently than I do. And kind of before reacting to people's tendencies, like they have a very strong position against something, being aware that there may be other things happening either with them or with me, and that may be biases or lack of awareness, lack of understanding.

When I asked Tracy about the role of the conversation in weakening unconscious biases, she shared how it added to her own perspective:

> So, it makes it more relatable when you hear a conversation in which other individuals are sharing experiences that may be similar to yours. You're like, "Oh. Okay. Yeah, I can directly relate to that." But even more is when they give you experiences that you haven't had. It totally adds a new dimension because you're like, "Oh, man. I never really thought about that." How that might have affected someone and which once again, if I ever run into that experience, now that I have more information and insight because I've heard someone else's experience with conversation. So instead of it being one person, like the facilitator giving me information, which is just a one-on-one exchange, now it's a conversation among people. So, it just broadens the experience and the learning.

In George's story, he was reacting to the social cue of a Black male, and from there he was inferring danger. By talking through the scenario with Tracy and Kalil, he was able to reflect on what actions he needed to take and create a plan: "Recognize that I have biases, recognize which biases I have. Use the Ladder of Inference to work on my biases and attempt to control them." He used the word "control" again in his final workshop reflection when talking about the training: "[It] expanded my realization of my biases, how to analyze and control." So, he went beyond just being aware of his biases to actually thinking about how to mitigate and control them, and in the future, he will use the Ladder of Inference to understand what data or social cue he is reacting to, so as to not make an incorrect inference again.

The value of the conversation for George and Tracy was different but equally important—both were transformational. For George, he was aware his story would exemplify racial bias, but he felt comfortable sharing and putting himself up for judgment, further showing his desire to change. For Tracy, it was more about being open to the perspective of others so that she could replace judgment with understanding. As she mentioned earlier, she was aware of the stereotype of Black males as threatening and aggressive,[25] but she still listened and tried to understand George's viewpoint.

Case Study: Mark and Denise

Here's another example of a transformational conversation between Mark, a White male, and Denise, an African-American female, both from the US. On the surface, these two seemed very far apart in terms of social identity. And their initial body language and words reinforced this impression. As they started their conversation, Denise was sitting back with her arms crossed over her chest, seemingly challenging Mark: "Okay, White male, what are you going to tell me about unconscious bias?"

Mark was unsure of how to proceed and was hesitant. However, Mark began by sharing his experience of starting a new career path recently in academia after spending thirty years in the IT industry. He felt he was being treated by the other professors as if this was his first job—"as a twenty-six-year-old." He was reluctant to call this bias until Denise encouraged him:

Denise: Yeah, you are a victim of it as well.

Mark: Yeah, no, definitely the victim of some bias. No. So, um, how does it make me feel? Very uncomfortable? Because again, they're putting me, as we just saw in the video, in a box I don't belong.

Denise: Right, exactly.

This was a turning point in the conversation. Denise leaned in and really listened, and she began to identify with Mark. She made a connection to herself as a manager and started using the collective pronoun, "our."

Denise: Wow. Very interesting, but you are probably being very effective with the students, right?

Mark: Yeah.

Denise: It's kind of like being in IT. I guess. I've been in there for a lot of years. But as, when I first joined this company, I got manager of the year, my first year. Yeah, I was just doing what I knew I was supposed to do . . . it's a thankless job.

Mark: Right.

Denise: Our, our rewards come from the inside. I mean, I call all this external stuff noise because it is. It will distract you.

Mark: Right.

Denise wrote this about her conversation with Mark:

> My partner discussion allowed me to learn about out-grouping. He gave a great example of out-grouping with his career. It opened more thinking and analyzing for me when interacting and observing situations. I will "rethink" making assumptions.

When I talked to Denise about the role of the conversations in the workshop, she said, "It helped a lot. You get to hear other stories, not just a lecture. You get to interact with the people and personalities."

Mark wrote the conversation gave him, "Confirmation of bias in my situation (me subject to bias) and that my efforts for feedback were appropriate (per the ladder)."

Denise validated his feelings and helped him make sense of the situation. Mark continued, "Well, I mean one way to make sense of something is to talk about it, right? So, if you can get people talking, it actually enables your sense-making abilities. And for them, when they hear other people talking, it may actually help them . . . moves the conversation forward."

For Mark and Denise, the conversation was valuable and helped weaken bias. With Mark, he felt validated and came to understand that everyone can experience bias. Denise realized this, as well, and began to question her own assumptions about race, gender, and bias.

Case study: Tony

Another surprising example of transformational conversation came from the workshop with the utility company I mentioned earlier. One of the gentlemen, Tony, shared his own story of bias—how he tended to overlook the younger guys and their abilities. He had been doing this job for thirty years, and he could do it better and faster than anyone around. But he said, "You know, I'm not doing those guys any favors by doing it all myself. They aren't learning, and I am not passing anything on to them. I'm doing them and the company a disservice. I need to give them the opportunities to try while I am around to help them."

In all these examples the participants experienced an "aha moment" in their conversations with someone else. It wasn't simply the shift in their own perspective that was brought about by hearing the story of another. It was also the telling of their own story that was transformational.

I received an email the day after the workshop from Tony that exactly articulated this, "I much enjoyed yesterday's class. It got us all to thinking and also talking about something that most likely would have never come up in our normal day-to-day conversations. We were still discussing the class and our individual biases this morning at the office."

The superintendent confirmed afterward that the workshop was a success for his team. He said the workshop was "one of the best training opportunities we have ever gone through. It opened up our minds to how unconscious bias affects us on a daily basis and took us way outside of our thinking box. My managers are still talking about the workshop."

I don't share that feedback to toot my own horn. I share it to further illustrate the power of transformational conversation. I could have strictly focused on knowledge share with the managers. I could have talked for the duration of the workshop and offered information on what unconscious bias is and how it impacts our decision (I do cover both), but I feel, and my research shows, that is it this conversational piece that is essential to change.

Refreeze

The final piece of the process model is refreeze.[26] So, now that we have unfrozen the undesired behavior and changed it, we want to refreeze the desired behavior. This must be a deliberate step and planned. We have to make an intentional effort to change by creating a plan we can stick with when our unconscious biases try to sway our behavior.

Research on implementation intentions has shown that through plans, we can begin to control our responses to undesirable influences.[27] Through our "coping plans," we can override our unconscious biases with deliberate conscious responses. Over time, we will decrease the influence of the unconscious bias and have more control over our behavior.[28,29,30,31]

Based on this research on implementation intentions, I ask participants to build upon their awareness and their transformational conversations to create a customized plan for what they will do differently, how they will implement change, and how they will hold themselves and others accountable. Specifically, I ask them:

- What will you start doing as a result of this workshop?
- What will you stop doing as a result of this workshop?
- What will you continue doing as a result of this workshop?

I encourage them to use if/then statements, so they have specific actions to take in a variety of scenarios.

And here are some examples of what other workshop participants will *start* doing:

Tracy said, "Review and refresh myself occasionally on bias literature to keep it conceptually in my field of view. Listen to my (and others') strong reactions to something to see if there is a bias acting out."

This could be written as: If I have a strong reaction to something or see someone else have a strong reaction to something, then I will listen to see if there is bias acting out.

Other participants wrote that they will "incorporate different perspectives and possibly rank them equally" and "share knowledge with others."

Let's look at some examples from workshop participants on what they will *stop* doing.

> Denise said, "So, I'm going to stop making assumptions. I said that, and I am going to start hearing. Because a lot of times I hear, 'Blah, blah, blah, blah, blah,' cause I've already gone to the end. I know what you're saying. And I've gone to the end. I don't say, 'Blah, blah, blah' out loud, but my brain is processing something else."

Her plan may look like this:

If I find that I am making assumptions about what another person is going to say, and I'm not actually listening (jumping to the end), then I will stop and really focus on the words the person is saying at that moment.

Another example specifically refers to the Ladder of Inference: "Stop making fast judgments and going up the ladder too fast."

This could be written as follows: If I find myself making fast judgments, then I will use the Ladder of Inference to help slow down my thinking and understand how I am processing data.

By asking the last question about what they "will continue to do," I am giving participants an opportunity to acknowledge what they are already doing well and to be intentional in their practice to continue this behavior.

The point really is to empower participants to create their own plans for dealing with unconscious bias and embolden them to practice what they learned in the classroom in the real world. I encourage them to post their plans in a prominent place, so they can see them often and refer to them daily.

The process model produced change

Looking at the data gathered from the reflections, pre-interviews, and post-interviews, all the participants experienced change, but the change was different in each person. In addition to the previous transformational change examples, the post-workshop interviews revealed a dramatic shift in thinking.

In her pre-workshop interview, Nancy described a diverse environment as "very peaceful" and working without any "colors and genders or anything around." She talked about "not seeing color" or addressing "that" in the workplace and her reluctance to "rock the boat" or "disturb the quiet." She had adopted a color-blind strategy—widely used in education, despite the lack of empirical evidence of it working.[32] In fact, research on this approach in elementary schools has actually demonstrated the opposite: having a "color-blind" mindset resulted in less detection of bias and less formal reporting of racial injustice.[33] The idea is "If you don't allow yourself to think about race, you can never be biased."[34] Nancy's color-blind mindset ignores the tension that can exist between ingroups and outgroups—specifically between white people and people of color and sets her up for unconscious racial bias.

Nancy's post-workshop interview reveals that her racial bias has weakened. She has abandoned her color-blind/racial bias and wants everyone to "feel open and free to share" and "be themselves." Most importantly, she feels "more empowered to go back to the workplace (and be aware) and consciously deal with bias on level two when needed," referring to Kahneman's System 2 functioning, which calls for slowing down and questioning assumptions.[35]

Kalil's pre-workshop interview revealed he had a very different idea about diversity than the six American participants in his workshop. He saw it as an advantage, and throughout the workshop, he seemed to have a difficult time relating to the personal impact of unconscious bias. However, in Kalil's post-workshop interview, he said the conversation piece of the workshop was extremely important because he had already seen a difference: "I have seen in myself a different way of handling things since that workshop day." He recalled an incident that happened because of something dangerous being found inside his children's school. The next day, his children did not want to go to school. His tendency is to confront what scares him, so, normally, he would have driven them to school himself and made them go in. However, this time Kalil decided to try to understand his children's perspective and listened as they told him how they would be distracted, looking out the windows, and unable to pay attention to their teachers. Fresh from the unconscious bias workshop, he was able look at the situation from his children's perspective and really hear what they were saying, and as a result, he let the children stay home that day. Kalil felt like this was a direct result of the workshop and laughed when he realized the change in himself.

When I conducted my initial study for my dissertation, my goal was to explore the extent to which a transformational conversation would engage people's social identity and weaken their implicit bias and support behavioral change. From my research, I found that this process can be effective, but it is effective in different ways for different people.

Transformational conversation goes beyond awareness. It gives participants an opportunity to receive feedback on their own experiences with unconscious bias and validates their feelings. Through listening to their partner's story about unconscious bias, the participants heard a different perspective and were able to employ empathy to identify with the other person and temporarily change their perspectives. This perspective shift through conversation is a valuable path to change.[36]

When I grouped workshop participants with someone of another gender, I thought this difference would be the defining feature of their unconscious bias stories, but that was not the case. The unconscious bias stories shared in the workshop included not just issues with gender and race, but differences in working styles, starting a new job, age, and culture. It was through transformational conversation that the participants began shifting from their own feelings to identifying with the other person and seeing commonalities, instead of only focusing on the differences.

Let's look at a few more examples of transformational conversation in a workshop setting. I held an unconscious bias workshop with an IT group of around hundred people with less than a third women, typical with my IT audiences. I had just brought the group back together after their breakout sessions sharing their own experiences of unconscious bias. As usual, I asked if anyone wanted to share their stories with the group. A middle-aged White gentleman midway in the auditorium turned to the woman next to him and asked if she minded him sharing their interaction. She nodded in the affirmative, and he proceeded to share:

> Susan told me about her experiences as a technical lead on projects with clients. She told me about a particular time when she went in to meet with the client, and he asked to speak with the technical lead. After she told him that was her, he said, "No, I mean the person who will handle the technical details of the IT solution." Again, she told him that was her, and he did not seem to believe her.

After recounting this scenario, the man said he was astonished this had happened to Susan. "I just cannot imagine a client doing this."

I looked around, and the other women were nodding in the room. They could relate to Susan's experience. But the fact that this man couldn't imagine this happening to him was very telling. He had never experienced this gender bias. As a male in the IT industry, he carried an authority bestowed upon him based strictly on his gender. Although women may have the same credentials, training, and experience, they still have to fight the stereotype that women are not technical.

I challenged the men in the room to talk to their female colleagues about this idea of questioned technical credibility. I knew Susan's experience was not an isolated example. Having spent twenty-plus years in the IT industry, I had witnessed this nearly every day and experienced it myself.

One participant in a workshop described having to have her ideas validated by a male colleague: "I will say something, and my team lead will turn to one of my male colleagues and ask if that's correct. He doesn't do that when my male colleagues say something." Again, there's a subtlety there. In this example, it's easy to say that it is a good idea to get other opinions. But the discrepancy is there, if you are aware—the female opinion has to be validated by a male.

Some of the women I spoke with felt they had to work harder or that their ideas weren't valued.

This idea of women not being seen as technical or competent has emerged in many of my workshops. And amazingly, the men are always shocked that this occurs. It's hard to imagine something that you have not experienced yourself. However, this is exactly the point of having transformational conversations. You hear about a perspective that is not your own. And for some it is incredible and shatters their reality.

Real-world settings of transformational conversations

It is one thing to have a transformational conversation in a workshop setting, but can it make a difference in a real-world situation? Consider these examples.

> Earlier in my career when I was as senior manager at the plant, I had this one guy who was suing the company, claiming he was unfairly passed over for a promotion. While all this is still tied up in litigation, he is on my shortlist for a promotion to a manager in my area. Now my thought is this guy hasn't shown me anything to make me believe he is management material. He is always bringing me his problems without any solutions.

> To me, that isn't a person I want to be a manager. But there was this lawsuit hanging out there, and my boss said to me, "Is Joe qualified for the job?"

I told him, "Yeah, but he isn't the person I want." He then basically told me I had to hire him anyway. I was mad because I didn't think he was management material. But I took him on and tried not to let the lawsuit or the sense of being forced to hire him influence the way I handled him. And I'll be damned if he didn't turn out to be one of the best managers I ever hired. When I talked to him about it later, he said that he didn't step up to the manager role until he had the role "there was no use acting like a manager, if I did not have the authority, title, or paycheck to go with it."

This experience changed the way I evaluated candidates and made me rethink my approach as a hiring manager.

The senior manager had made assumptions about the employee based on her previous experiences with him—he was not "management material." However, through a conversation with the guy, her thinking was transformed. She now understood his perspective.

In her seminal book, *Caste*, Isabel Wilkerson speaks about a transformational conversation she had with a plumber from the dominant caste—a White male. Wilkerson talks about the initial meeting with the plumber who she called to fix a leak in her basement. The plumber is taken aback at first because she is a Black woman in a predominantly white neighborhood, and he asks for the lady of the house. When she tells him that she is the lady of the house, he reluctantly follows her to the basement and watches her fumble around with boxes, looking for the drain. He was very stand-offish and seemed to have no interest in troubleshooting the problem. Because of Wilkerson's deep insight into the caste system and her experiences, in her words, as part of the "lower caste," she sought to bridge the gap with her words and "threw a Hail Mary at his humanity."[37]

My mother just died last week, I told him. "Is your mother still alive?"

He looked down at the wet floor. "No . . . no, she isn't."

Somehow, I sensed that already, which is why I brought it up.

"She died in 1991," he said. "She was fifty-two years old."

"That's not old at all," I said.

"No, she wasn't. My father's still alive, he's seventy-eight. He's in a home south of here. My sister lives nearby to him."

"You're lucky to still have your father," I said.

"Well, he's mean as they come."

I contemplated the significance of that. What might his father have exposed him to when it comes to people who look like me? But I kept it to the present.[38]

Wilkerson continues the story with the two finding common ground in the loss of their mothers. Through conversation, Wilkerson builds a bridge between her and the plumber. And as the space between them begins to narrow figuratively, the plumber begins to search for the source of the leak and physically help Wilkerson.

I will give one final example before we move on. Most of us by now know what mansplaining is, but for those who don't, I will offer a definition. It is when a woman says something, and a man turns right around and says the exact same thing, usually in similar wording. Sometimes he thinks he is helping to clarify, "I think what you mean to say is . . ." Or it could be the man doesn't consciously realize he is saying what he just heard from the woman. This makes it even more infuriating because he will present the idea like it his own original idea. And the woman is sitting there thinking, "I just said that."

When I was in graduate school at Georgia State, another student in my cohort did this regularly. One day, after he had just rephrased something I had said for the second or third time that day, I told two of my female friends in my cohort that I was going to call him out on his mansplaining. They discouraged me. They said he wouldn't care or believe he was doing it. He would be dismissive. I disagreed. I didn't think he was aware he was doing it.

I was right. Later in the day when I asked him if he knew he had been mansplaining, he seemed surprised. He did not know what the word meant and asked me for an example. I had several to share with him. He thanked me and asked me to call him out if I saw him doing it again.

He wasn't aware. I brought it to his attention, and we had a conversation. That doesn't mean he won't offend again, but when he does, he has a new association in his head—I think I'm doing what Kim called me out on. And now, it's his choice. He can choose to keep on with his mansplaining—letting his unconscious stay in control. Or he can choose to be more thoughtful and deliberate and monitor his behavior until it becomes a permanent change.

In most cases of unconscious bias, there must be some work done. Transformational conversation is not always going to happen in the heat of the moment. It may take an outside intervention—a training or an opportunity for the person to slow down to understand another's perspective. This is why the three-step model is important.

Sometimes, we are talking about a behavior that is so ingrained in the person that they don't know it exists. That is how unconscious biases work—we react without thinking deeply. To unfreeze a behavior, you start with awareness—what are unconscious biases and how might they show up? This starts the gears of participants working. They begin to make connections with the examples of unconscious bias and start to filter through their own experiences. This flows nicely into the change behavior. Why change? Because they have been exposed to another perspective through transformational conversation. The conversation and learning about how unconscious bias impacts another person begins to transform their thinking. And then the key is to refreeze this new way of thinking, so the person begins to remodel their behavior almost on demand as they practice perspective shifting throughout their day. And with time, the hope is that the unconscious bias is weakened, and a huge red flag signaling for the person to slow down is triggered in situations where bias can occur.

In the next chapter we will talk about creating an inclusive culture where transformational conversations can occur, and diverse voices can be heard.

Chapter takeaways

- Research shows that contact between people decreases prejudice. Transformational conversation is based on contact theory and taps into empathy as a change agent.

- The process model focuses on unfreezing the unconscious bias by bringing awareness to it. Change is brought about through transformational conversation. And refreeze involves planning for future interactions—practicing how to short-circuit the bias.

- The ladder of inference can help you slow down and recognize where biases may have influenced your thinking, decision-making, or behavior.

- The bias feedback loop encourages you to seek out further feedback to either contradict or confirm your perspective.

CHAPTER 5

CREATE A CULTURE
OF INCLUSION.

Goal: Give readers help to create a culture of inclusion.

When I was still a junior employee at IBM, I was in a meeting with a roomful of executives. As a writer in executive comms, I often attended high-level meetings. There was one female in the room full of men. She was dressed in a bold red suit, and I admired her confidence. As the meeting was ending, I began to gather up the coffee cups to throw them away. She placed her hand on mine to still it, "Don't ever clean up after them. They won't see you on their level." I have kept this message in my head for decades, remembering that in some spaces my "place" is dictated by the majority. However, now, I make an effort to take up space. I speak up when I want, and I don't feel relegated to occupy the space "designated" for me.

When I told this story a few years ago to the MBA class I was teaching, one my students, a White male, immediately started to object, "I don't think that's the case with women in business . . ." I stopped him, actually putting up my hand in a physical gesture of "Stop." I asked him two questions: "Are you a female?" and "Are you me?"

Of course, he answered no to both. I told him unless this was a shared experience, he had no standing to negate or doubt my experience or that of the executive. This is too often what we do. We start to object, refute, or completely dismiss someone else's experience when it does not match our own reality—which is, of course, of our own creation. The correct response is to listen without interrupting—every single time.

What is inclusion?

Unconscious bias training should be one of the tools used to create a diverse environment. But a diverse workplace, organization, or community alone should not be the end objective. We should be striving to build an inclusive culture full of diverse people.

What's the difference, you might ask? The difference is in the reception. An inclusive environment is one where diversity is not only welcome but appreciated. We don't want to use diversity to check a box or meet a quota. We want diversity to broaden our circle, to include more perspectives, and to create something stronger and more innovative than we could with a homogenous group. Inclusion reshapes the status quo through diversity. Inclusion says, "Yes, come as you are. We do not ask you to conform. We actually would like you to transform our current culture to be broader and more equal." Inclusion has to be deliberate at first before it can evolve organically. Throwing a bunch of diverse folks together does not build an inclusive culture. In fact, it can do the opposite, if there is not a true investment of time, resources, and leadership on the front end.

We talked in Chapter 3 about making sure to hire diverse candidates—not just people like ourselves (similarity bias). But you have to do more than just hire diverse individuals together and expect magic to happen. You must actively create an inclusive culture where everyone can thrive. This chapter is about giving you the information and tools to help create that inclusive environment.

True self

If I bring my true self to work, how will I be perceived? For many, this is a question they ask themselves every single day. Should I put a picture of my same-sex partner on my desk? What will happen if I wear my natural hair to the office? Can I slip out of the office four times a day to say my prayers?

If I leave early to watch my child's baseball game, will I be perceived as less committed?

Why would we want our employees, colleagues, friends, or family torturing themselves with these questions? At what cost to productivity are we asking those around us to cover or hide their true selves?

Darnel refers to his partner as his roommate in mixed company. A childhood friend tells me she is gay but asks me not to tell another mutual friend because the friend is a conservative. A child declares he is an atheist, but his mother urges him not to tell any of his classmates because they live in the "Bible Belt South."

All these descriptions are built upon the unconscious biases and in some cases, conscious biases, in our society. Everyone is playing a role—the role they think is expected of them. For Darnel and my childhood friend, they don't think they will be accepted. But acceptance is really the wrong word. They fear they will be judged if they are their true selves, so they present what is expected of them. This fear is not unfounded and is often reinforced when they try to venture outside their societal box. For the mother who fears her child will be rejected by his classmates for being an atheist, there is also a bit of fear for herself that she will be seen as an ungodly woman.

For some reading this, you may have been the one placed in a box you don't belong in. Most likely, we all have at some point in our lives. Think about how that made you feel. I know from my own experience that it doesn't feel very good. As you read through this chapter, keep that feeling in mind, especially when you find yourself feeling defensive or questioning the validity of some of the examples or suggestions. This chapter is about preventing that feeling of unfairness. It is about taking steps to make others feel welcomed, heard, and valued. This starts with listening.

Listening generously

Listening is both the easiest and hardest way to create inclusion. We have all had that experience when we are having a great conversation with someone and really connecting, and time just seems to fly by. You may feel you are the only two people on earth. And we have all had a conversation where the other person is distracted, checking their phone, and looking around. Think about how each of these types of conversations make you feel.

I have a mentor who is near the top of the rungs in a Fortune 500 company and has a massive responsibility as chief spokesperson for the company. Yet, every time I have a meeting or call with him, he puts everything aside to concentrate on me. He asks, "What can I do to help you today?" I always leave our meetings feeling like the most important person in the world. That is the feeling I try to create for others, but it's not easy.

Most of us don't listen to hear. We listen to respond. As the other person is speaking, we are thinking of what we will say next. Or we may be mentally arguing with what they are saying—ready to pounce on any inconsistency or challenge to our own beliefs.

Listening asks us to constantly check our own thoughts and concentrate on the words of the person addressing us. Instead, we are often multi-tasking, but we still insist we are listening, even though our body language says otherwise. Sometimes we are evaluating the person's appearance instead of listening. So, what's the answer? We have to slow down and tell ourselves to focus. Shut System 1 down—the one yelling at us, "Yes, we have heard this before. I know what to say. I don't need to listen anymore. I know where this is going."

Remember the earlier example of the workshop participant who heard, "Blah, blah, blah . . ." when talking to someone? She said she had already skipped to the end and assumed where they were going. In her plan, she wrote that her goal is to really listen and not skip to the end. I think this is a good goal for all of us.

If you are interrupting, you are not listening. You have been planning your response. Sure, the person may trigger thoughts in your head, and it may be okay to share if you are in a brainstorming session. But try to consider the space around a person's thoughts as sacred—something you don't want to intrude upon. Give them time to talk. If you think you will forget your thought, write it down. And when they are done, it is your turn. I call this listening generously.

Also, make sure you are not discounting what the other person is saying by trying to defend or deflect. For example, if someone is telling you how they felt a joke your colleague told was offensive, listen. This is not the time to say, "Oh, I don't think Joe meant anything by it. You are taking it too seriously. It was a joke." Don't make the person feel as if their feelings are invalid. The proper response is to listen and try to see the perspective of the other person. You do not have a right to tell someone else how they should feel.

I was recently at the doctor, and she had a medical student shadowing her. After the doctor asked if it was okay for the student to stay for the exam, the student began peppering me with questions about my symptoms. I could tell he wasn't listening to my answers. His lack of follow-up questions showed that. He was just trying to get through his checklist of questions—going through the systems of the body. Unfortunately, this meant he was more focused on himself than me. He was not listening generously.

Return to civility

In the last few years, I have seen a tremendous uptick in my requests for "Civility in the Workplace" seminars or workshops. There is an urgency expressed that can almost be described as desperation. CEOs, HR, and Learning Professionals are trying to ratchet down the strong, one-sided rhetoric that has replaced healthy discussions and disagreements. Work conflict is now following the example set in politics of no compromise, no negotiation, and no willingness to hear a different perspective.

Transformational conversations as a tool to ensure participants understand the perspective of another person can help us return to civility through listening. The key is to be able to step outside yourself and really struggle to see the point of view of someone whom you perceive as different. I use the word struggle intentionally. The ability to really listen without coming up with your own arguments against what the person is saying, to think about what you want to say next, or to not just shut down completely is difficult. It's a constant struggle within your brain to make sure you are fully present in System 2 thinking, being very conscious. This is the only way to ensure your unconscious biases are not overtaking the conversation. Our tendency is to focus on only the points that reinforce our own arguments (confirmation bias), ones that reaffirm that the two of us have nothing in common (similarity bias), or even slipping into dismissing the other's point of view because this person is not part of our group, so they couldn't possibly understand (ingroup/outgroup bias).

The overriding factor is all these examples is the need to listen generously. You must decide at the onset of the discussion that you will fully focus on the other person's perspective. You will need to eliminate distractions and stay emotionally neutral. This will require empathy—a shift from judgment to understanding. You cannot shout the other person down, refuse to listen, or even ridicule their speech.

This does not mean you have to agree, but you do have to give the other person equal airtime. After the other person has expressed their opinion, you can calmly tell them where you differ or even better, where you are on similar terms. If this is a work decision and there is no middle ground, invite a neutral party to give feedback.

If this is strictly a personal discussion, agree to disagree. There does not have to be a winner and loser in every discussion. We are social creatures, so we naturally seek out the company of other humans. Unfortunately, we have been taught to not have conversations about potentially volatile topics, such as politics and religion. This censoring of topics has left us without a framework for having these discussions. Consequently, we shift to defensive rhetoric when our views are challenged.

So, here's your framework for handling listening and having a civil conversation:

1. *Eliminate distractions.* Make sure you are not allowing your System 1 thinking (made up your unconscious biases) to be in charge. That means no multi-tasking.

2. *Really listen.* Don't think about your counterpoints or dismiss what the person is saying.

3. *Employ empathy.* Try to put yourself in the other person's shoes and understand the motivation behind their viewpoint.

4. *Be respectful.* Just because you don't agree with someone does not give you the right to negate or rudely dismiss their point of view.

5. *Share your perspective.* If you have followed point three above, you should have empathy flowing between you and the other person. This is a good opportunity to share your opinion without demanding the other person adopt your perspective.

6. *Agree to disagree.* If you have been following each step, each of you has now engaged in a transformational conversation. Agreement is not important Hopefully, you have considered a different viewpoint, and that's all that is necessary.

7. *Part amicably.* Just because you do not agree with someone, that does not mean you should be uncivil. Thank the person for sharing and leave an opportunity for follow-up.

Again, I am not saying this is easy. It will be a struggle at first. Disagreements are naturally going to happen in our multi-connected world. However, we don't have to allow every disagreement to escalate to a war of words. In the next chapter, we will talk about when to walk away when conversation does not work.

Meetings

The instruction on listening extends to meetings. Sometimes it can be difficult to be inclusive in meetings. You may just want to get through it quickly and move on. But if you are short on time, you must work even harder to slow down. And if you have an uncomfortable topic to discuss, make sure you set aside enough time to allow others to be heard. Our tendency is to try to move quickly to get it over with. I did this recently with my non-profit board. I was anxious to get a decision on a complicated legal matter, so we could move on with our plans. I did not take the time to consult with the board before I acted. I didn't make a conscious decision to not consult them, but I imagined that consulting with anyone else would slow me down. And I didn't want that. A board member called me out on this, and I had to acknowledge he was 100 percent correct. I hadn't made a conscious effort to exclude them, but I had.

Part of inclusion is also making sure that you don't let your meetings be overtaken by an extrovert or a person who likes to hear themselves talk. Some people like to take you forcefully down their stream of consciousness—completely oblivious to whether you are willingly or unwillingly along for the ride. They don't realize they are dominating the conversation, so you have to act as a moderator for the sake of the other meeting members. Most of the time, you know who these people are before the meeting starts, so you can be ready with a polite, but firm, way to redirect: "Jack, that is definitely a unique way of looking at the problem, but I would like to hear some other opinions on the matter." Or "I'm afraid we haven't scheduled enough time in this meeting to go that deep into the issue or give it the attention it deserves; can you and I schedule some time to talk this through?" And then make sure you do set a follow-up time, or the person will feel slighted and continue to highjack future meetings.

You can also have the opposite problem of having a person who rarely speaks up in a meeting. There are a couple of ways to deal with this, depending on the personality of the person and your group. You can call on the person by name and ask a question: "Lisa, what do you think about that?" But this can sometimes make the person feel that they have been put on the spot and cause embarrassment. I recommend another approach—especially if you are in a larger group. Approach the person individually and praise their opinion or perspective. For example, during a workshop I had, a gentleman didn't say anything during the first part of the session. He was listening, but he wasn't taking part in the discussion. I went over to him during the break and asked him what he thought about the class so far. He had a very thoughtful answer, "I am learning a lot about how to recognize my own biases." And then he gave a specific example of confirmation bias. I praised him for his ability to make the connection and asked him if he would mind sharing his example with the class. This was the confidence boost he needed. He not only shared his story with the class, but he enthusiastically added more to the rest of the class discussion. He just needed a little encouragement and recognition.

This example can be replicated in a workplace environment. Hold a pre-call or meeting with the reticent individual—just the two of you. Ask their opinion about a particular topic and legitimately thank them for the input. And then ask them to share that input in the meeting with the others. If you find the person still does not speak up in the meeting, you may have to prompt them: "Crystal and I were speaking earlier about this issue, and she had a really great point on the budget for the project. Crystal, will you share what we talked about with the team?" You have offered some validation for Crystal's viewpoint and given her the opening to participate.

Also, make sure to send out the agenda ahead of the meeting. This allows others to think about the topics beforehand, gather information, provide additional topics, and contribute during the meeting. You want participants to switch from thinking it is "your" agenda to thinking of it as "our" agenda. You want the meeting to be a rich discussion, instead of a reporting session. If your participants don't know what the topics are, they will not come prepared. They may still be thinking about your previous agenda item as you move on to the next one.

Sending the agenda in advance also helps someone who may have low vision. They can print it out in a larger font or magnify it on their screen.

Allow pauses. This is the same as with all conversations. We are usually uncomfortable with long pauses, but this may be exactly what the other person needs—time to think. So, don't rush to fill the silence.

I also make a point to scan the faces of the participants to look for signs of confusion or disagreement. If you are on a call where you can't see everyone, you may need to say, "Anu, I haven't heard from you on this issue. What is your opinion?"

And lastly on this point, make sure you are not talking too quickly if you have an international group. For some, they may be listening to what you are saying, translating it to their native language, and then translating it back to the original language for a reply. This is another instance where pauses are great.

Language

Language can signal whether you are inclusive. I was talking with a client, conducting an intake assessment to see how I could help him. He said, "We no doubt need some help in the HR area, but I think we have this diversity and inclusion thing covered. I mean, when we speak with the salesmen, we talk to them about how to interact with women—you know, they control most of the buying decisions." And here's a case of the sneaky unconscious bias creeping into conversation. I quietly reminded him he had women in sales also and suggested he use "salespeople" going forward. His reply, "Well, that's sort of our broad term, so you know what I mean."

I do know what he means. As a woman, I hear this type of argument of "maleness as the neutral, general term." I don't buy it. I don't feel included when someone addresses the room with a "How are you guys doing?" I don't feel included when someone calls me chairman of the board—chairperson is the neutral here. And I don't like to hear people being dismissive by saying I'm being too literal. Language is important. It can divide us or connect us. And using the proper language for your audience is part of addressing the whole group—not just the guys, but the other half of the room and those who identify as gender neutral.

Use inclusive language. Try "you all," "folks," or "people," instead of gender-specific language. Yes, it does take a little more work to break this habit based on years of not thinking about it. But once you make a conscious effort to change, it will become easier. And really, it is such a simple shift in thinking.

I remember a payroll specialist coming in to talk with a room full of HR professionals, who all happened to be women. He used "guys" in almost every other sentence. He could clearly see we were all women, but he continued to refer to the women as "guys." Written out like this it seems rather ridiculous. Was he being intentionally rude by using "guys?" No, I don't think he was, and when I talked to him afterward and pointed out his language, he was deeply embarrassed. However, this was not my goal. The last thing I would want to do is shame someone. I know from the research that shaming as a catalyst for change does not work with unconscious bias. I wanted him to be aware of his constant use of "guys" and to think about how he could better connect with his audience. I suspect he will use "guys" again in future demonstrations, but I am also sure he will at one point pause and correct himself. From there, he can start to build a new habit—one that he does not have to consciously think about every time.

Using inclusive language also means being aware of someone else's preferences, such as pronoun usage. Gender-neutral and inclusive pronouns, such as they and them, may be preferable for some. Respect these preferences and remember them. If you make a mistake, apologize. If you are unsure, ask. And you can show your support by including and stating your own preferred pronouns.

Recruitment

Do you use inclusive language in your hiring practices? In addition to the direction in Chapter 3, I would also encourage you to look at the language in your recruitment ads, your online postings, and the general descriptions about your company and culture. Will the language attract the person you wish to employ?

Research has shown that women respond more favorably toward advertisements that feature "female-coded words" associated with teamwork and agreement, such as committed, cooperative, dependable, honest, interpersonal, loyal supporter, and understanding. Contrast these with words typically featured on recruitment sites: risk-taker, adventurous, confident, decisive, driven, independent, and opinionated. Researchers call these "masculine-coded words," and they will keep a woman from applying for a job. However, men don't respond negatively to the female-coded words, so it makes sense to use language that will attract a broader audience through inclusive language.[1]

There are several tools available to help you check for masculine-codes words in ads, such as the Gender Decoder for Job Ads.[2]

Language affects perception

Inclusive language goes beyond good recruitment practice. Your language affects both how you see and how you are seen. American linguist Benjamin Whorf suggested our words determine what we see and that language influences thought.[3]

Research from Jennifer Eberhardt, a social psychologist at Stanford, proved this theory. She had participants look at a racially ambiguous male face. Eberhardt told one group the male was Black and the other group he was White. She then asked each group to draw the man as they looked at the picture of the man. The group who was told that the man was Black drew stereotypical features on the man, such as a broad nose, large lips, and curly hair. The group who was told the man was White drew none of those exaggerated features. Eberhardt's suggestion on race changed the participants' perception.[4]

Here's another example:

In a study conducted in the early 1980s, John Darley and Paget Gross conducted research to find out how a person's socioeconomic status influences others' perception of that person. The researchers showed participants a video of a girl taking an academic test and asked them to speculate on her academic ability. Those who were told she had a high socioeconomic status rated her as having above average academic ability. Those who were told she had a low socioeconomic status rated her as having a below average academic ability.[5]

In both examples, words or labeling triggered unconscious biases in the participants and influenced their perceptions.

Language reflects on you

Your language can also impact how you are perceived—negatively or positively. Let's look at a few examples.

As I was waiting for my monthly allergy shot, I heard the nurse refer to herself as the "R" word because she had absentmindedly forgotten one of the steps to check a patient in. I flinched, but I was far away from her, so she wouldn't have noticed.

She then went on to say loudly enough for the whole waiting room to hear, "I am the driver of the short bus today."

If you do not know what either of these means, she was trying to mock herself as dimwitted by comparing herself to a person with a cognitive disability.

A woman close to me laughed and looked to me to join her. I did not. I have a son who has a cognitive impairment. Her language was a painful reminder to me that some find his disability a clever joke.

Before you write this section off as trying to enforce political correctness, I will remind you that the topic of this chapter is creating an inclusive culture. Language that alienates even one person will not help you achieve that, so stick with me. I will give you two more examples before I move on to some tips on how to create this culture.

I was participating in a lively discussion in class when one of my classmates said he felt "gypped." I closed my eyes and decided to let it go. I was already known as that "diversity and inclusion gal" to the person who made the comment, so I wasn't expecting a positive outcome if I said anything. But then someone else in the class used the same word a few minutes later—someone who should have known better. This made me angry—not at the first person because he was known for not thinking before he spoke. And I wasn't upset at the second person either. I was angry with myself. I had decided to let the first derogatory reference to the Romani people go unchecked.[6] As a result, it was normalized, and it spread. I had witnessed it firsthand. I took a deep breath and calmly told the class why the phrase was unacceptable and offensive. There were a lot of, "I never really thought about what it meant. You hear it so often." Now, they know, and I don't expect to hear it from that group again.

I will share one final extreme example, so you get the point. Terence Crutcher, Sr. was a forty-year-old father and Black. According to news accounts, 911 callers reported a car in the middle of the street with the driver door open and the engine still running and blocking traffic. The Tulsa police said when they arrived on the scene, they found Crutcher walking toward his vehicle and refusing to show his hands. One officer used a taser on him, and the other officer subsequently shot him. Video footage shows Crutcher with his hands in the air. He was unarmed.

Shortly before Crutcher was shot, police officers in the helicopter on the scene could be heard saying over the police radio, "That looks like a bad dude, too, could be on something." Did the words, "bad dude" influence Officer Betsy Jo Shelby to shoot Crutcher? We will never know. Officer Shelby likely doesn't know herself. But let's look at the situation. She is dealing with an unknown male in a seemingly escalating situation. She is stressed, functioning on adrenaline, and operating in System 1—the fast-acting part of the brain. Her limbic system has taken over—fight or flight? This does not excuse her for shooting an unarmed man, but it does offer a possible example of the immense power of words to influence. His family agreed. Crutcher's sister said later in a press conference,

"You all want to know who that big, bad dude was? That big, bad dude was my twin brother. That big, bad dude was a father. That big, bad dude was a son. That big, bad dude was enrolled at Tulsa Community College—just wanting to make us proud. That big, bad dude loved God. That big, bad dude was at church, singing, with all his flaws, every week."[7]

Language matters.

What can you do?

I held a workshop with a company that managed low-income housing. The HR VP asked me to come talk about language and wanted me to emphasize to the employees that impactful role they each one had in creating a community of respect and inclusion. Her words: "Society has placed a certain stigma on low-income housing and the people who reside there. But low income does not equal low quality. Our employees have to overcome their own unconscious bias to provide quality, fair, compassionate service to our residents."

I will close this section on language and perception with the advice I gave to these employees:[7]

Know the impact unconscious bias has on you. It affects your decision-making ability. It influences the way you perceive the world. And it changes the way you treat those around you.

Think before you label or stereotype. Re-evaluate where your information about the group came from. Get to know the individual.

Be open. Learn about other individuals from diverse backgrounds that may be unfamiliar to you.

Extremes on inclusion

I would be remiss if I didn't caution you on going to an extreme with inclusion. Being inclusive is not the same as ignoring differences. Each person is unique, and to ignore that is both delusional and dismissive.

I'll share an example. I facilitated a workshop with a hundred plus women who were engineers. We were discussing cognitive biases that can influence our decision making. A White woman at a front table, (I will call her Jane), raised her hand and said, "I don't see color. I treat everyone the same." I thought the African American woman sitting at her table, (I will call her Lisa), was going to jump out of her seat in reaction to this remark. I thanked Jane for sharing her thoughts. Then, I turned to Lisa and asked, "Do you have a different opinion?"

She calmly said, "I do. That is ridiculous to say you don't see color. Here I am, right in front of you. You can see my skin is darker than yours. You can't ignore my Blackness."

The exchange continued. Jane looked briefly uncomfortable and surprised, but quickly added, "I thought that is what I was supposed to do. I was raised to not see color." Lisa replied, "No. You can see difference, acknowledge it, and then appreciate it."

As if watching a tennis match, all eyes turned to Jane. She seemed confused for a few minutes, and the room was silent. And then she spoke, "Thank you. No one has ever told me that before."

And just like that, we continued with our workshop. Jane and Lisa had given the group a gift—a sincere exchange about race—insight into the thoughts of two seemingly different people. And they had done it with full emotion but with respect and curiosity. It was a credit to both women that they didn't react defensively. They both shared their perspectives openly, and the whole group was able to benefit.

Allies

My last point on creating an inclusive environment is that we need allies, so we must create training that appeals to everyone. Some of the worst diversity training I have seen focused on shaming. You have probably seen it too—the White males in the room with their arms crossed against their chests as a visible barrier to engagement. We can't walk into a room with an air of superiority and expect to influence. We only make our audience defensive, and communication is stopped before it even starts.[8]

The literature is clear that shaming the dominant group is not effective. For those in the majority/dominant group, they may not even be aware that their biases are impacting those in the minority group. And because the biases may even be beneficial to the dominant group, there is little motivation to change.[9] As a result, focusing on this dynamic will be challenging and perhaps uncomfortable for the participants in the workshop, as Linnehan et al. argue:

> The influence that racial identity has on people's motivation to engage in the types of behaviors consistent with a pluralistic organization may depend on group membership. Those who strongly identify with the dominant group's culture are likely to be comfortable in the traditional working environment predominated by values of White, able-bodied, heterosexual men.[10] As such, they may see little reason for the organization to develop a more pluralistic culture.[11]

In other words, the White males are going to be more satisfied with the status quo and less likely to be open to change. In addition, Linnehan et al. point out, "Members of dominant groups may believe that prejudice, stereotyping, and discrimination do not exist.[12,13] They may feel wrongly accused by efforts to raise awareness of these issues.[14] Finally, they simply may be unwilling to recognize that their success is partly a result of their unearned advantages."[15,16]

Lai and Nosek, social psychologists at the University of Virginia, "analyzed eighteen different strategies to see which are the most effective for addressing unconscious bias." They found that "exhaustive efforts to get people in the dominant group to understand the plight of people in non-dominant groups can often create a greater sense of difference between the groups and . . . reduce the sense of connection and empathy to the 'out group.'"[17] Put more plainly—those in the dominant/ingroup may feel their social identity is being challenged and see diversity training as a threat and punitive. "This is one of the reasons there is such strong white male backlash around diversity and inclusion issues. White men are reacting to being blamed and 'made' to feel guilty for things they often don't realize that they're doing, or for privileges they don't realize they have had for longer than any of them have been alive."[18]

Shaming often takes the form of focusing on historical prejudice. In simplistic terms we would say, "White males are responsible for all that is wrong with the world."

I will point out the obvious. White men are disproportionally represented in senior and executive positions in most US organizations. Again, if you come into a class pointing fingers, you will immediately put your audience on the defensive. White men "may feel targeted and offended by the implication that they could be prejudiced."[19] In addition, you may imply that only White males have bias, which is not true.

Again, this brings us back to the unhelpful push that White males need to be shamed into change. You must look at your overall goal—what do you want to accomplish? I think of this as any conversation—you must first connect with your partner before they can hear you. They have to hear you to be motivated to change. If someone is in a defensive posture, they are not open to hearing you.

There is a definite place for bringing in past and even current wrongs, but you must understand your audience and your goals. I often come back to these two—audience and goals—to center myself. I am an empath, so I get angry and upset about all injustices. But I go back to my goal—change. And ask myself, "How I can affect change?"

I know from the research I can't do it with shame and painting the entire White male population as biased. We cannot exclude 60 percent to 70 percent of the workforce in some industries and expect to make any change in the makeup of the employee base. What do I mean by exclude? I mean to isolate them and shame them for their gender and race. We need male allies to help with inclusion.

Given the chance, people want to do the right thing and work in a diverse, equitable, and inclusive environment. But if cornered, the human tendency is to create an "us vs them" mentality. For this inclusion to occur, we need a diverse set of voices at the table. However, we need to make sure we have created an environment for that diversity to flourish. Inclusion is about creating space for all individuals to thrive—regardless of their race, socioeconomic status, sexual preference, gender identity, disability, or any other perceived difference. I love the saying, "Y'all means all."

Chapter takeaways

- Unconscious bias training is a tool and should be used in conjunction with a robust diversity, equity, and inclusion strategy.

- Strive to create an environment where everyone can be their "true selves" without worrying if they will be accepted or included.

- Listen generously. Listen to hear and not to respond. Don't think about what you will say next, interrupt, or argue silently with the speaker. Hear their words.

- To listen generously and have a civil conversation: (1) Eliminate distractions, (2) Really listen without arguing or dismissing, (3) Employ empathy, (4) Be respectful, (5) Share your perspective, (6) Agree to disagree, and (7) Part amicably.

- Use inclusive language that is not gender specific. Learn and respect the pronoun preferences of those who you interact with.

- Language can influence perception, so think carefully about your word choices.

- A strong, inclusive culture needs allies. Make sure you are not alienating potential allies through shaming.

CHAPTER 6.

KNOW WHEN TO WALK AWAY.

Goal: Enable readers to recognize when to engage and when to withdraw.

I was in an online meeting when an acquaintance responded to a question from one of the other participants: "I know this is in no way politically correct, but I am going to say it anyway."

In general, if you catch yourself uttering this phrase, "I know that this is not politically correct . . ." you should just stop talking. And in this case, the man should have stopped himself. Unfortunately, he proceeded to describe a scenario where only White women could be the saviors of the children with rare disease. This is an often-used trope in literature and movies (e.g., The Help, The Blind Side, Freedom Writers). If you aren't sure what I am talking about, see the next chapter for other books to read and do your homework.

I took a deep breath and looked around the squares of the other people participating in the call for a reaction. No one seemed to blink. Should I say something now or wait? I could feel the anger rising in me, so I was pretty sure I was not going to be kind with my admonishment. So, I let it go and mentally planned to follow up.

As I calmed down, I began to think more carefully about what I would do and say. And you know what? I decided it would not make a bit of difference to discuss the incident with the gentleman. He had signaled he knew what he said was not right, but he said it anyway. He was very conscious of his bias and seemed to almost embrace it.

We will talk more about how to react to incidents such as this using the RISK model in the following pages.

When conversation doesn't work

Sometimes when you try to talk to someone about unconscious bias, it is not going to go well. The person may be defensive and try to gloss over their behavior or speech:

> "You have me all wrong." "You are misinterpreting what I said." "That's not what I meant." "That's not what I said."

Or they may be belligerent and start to attack you to make you feel bad about bringing it up:

> "You are being oversensitive." "I don't care about being politically correct." "Whatever happened to free speech?"

Either way, it will become pretty clear to you that no amount of conversation is going to move the needle with the person when it comes to unconscious bias. For whatever reason, they are determined to stay stuck on their own perspective and refuse to see an alternative one.

And sometimes you are dealing with conscious bias—meaning the person has chosen to be biased—and you may just have to walk away. It is not your responsibility to educate someone else on unconscious bias. You need to determine if it is safe for you mentally, physically, and professionally to proceed with the conversation. In the immortal words of Kenny Rogers, "You need to know when to walk away and when to run." Using the RISK model will help with this.

RISK model

The RISK model of response follows four steps that correspond to each letter of the word "risk."

Risk: What are the risks to me if I respond?

Important: Is it important for me to respond?

Stay Open: Stay open to the other person's perspective.

Keep Calm: If it didn't go well, keep calm.

What are the risks?

As with any situation, we should weigh the risks before we act. Ask yourself these questions:

- If I respond to what I feel is unconscious bias toward me or another, what risks do I face? Is the person I need to talk with my boss or supervisor, or does she/he have any direct power over me?

- If I escalate the situation, am I likely to have a friendly ear or a defensive one?

- Should I say something immediately? Are there risks to responding right away? Do I need to wait until I cool down? Should I wait until I can talk to the person one-on-one?

- Can I voice my concerns in a way that is understandable to the other person—not completely without emotion, but not so overwhelmed with emotion that the other person shuts down?

Remember the Ladder of Inference? It's a great tool to use to check your own assumptions about a situation. You can walk yourself back down the ladder to make sure you have chosen the right data and not based your assumptions on faulty rungs.

Is it important?

Before responding, we need to think about how important it is for us to respond.

Ask yourself,

- Is this a one-off situation, or have I encountered this multiple times with this person?

- Will my saying something make a difference? This could be a difference in how you feel about the situation, or it could mean triggering a change in the other person.

- Do you have to maintain an ongoing relationship with the person—for work, for family harmony, etc.? Do you need there to be a changed behavior for future interactions? In other words, will this person's behavior impact your ability to complete your work?

Stay open to the other person

If you have decided in the last step that the conversation is important, go into it with an open mind. Assume best intentions. Going in with an accusatory tone will not further the conversation. If you are going in throwing allegations, then the relationship must not be that important to you, so you should not proceed. You have already made up your mind.

Start with "I" statements instead of "you" statements. "I feel this . . ." "What I heard you say in the meeting is . . ." "I felt frustrated in the meeting because I did not feel my concerns were being addressed." Be as specific as you can. "I felt insulted when you asked Marcus why his numbers weren't as good as mine. I felt it implied that you were downplaying my abilities to excel by implying that naturally Marcus should be doing better than me."

We will have a tendency at this point to lay out a litany of grievances. But before we go off on a diatribe, it's important to stop and allow the other person to respond. If a person feels they are being attacked, they will go into defense mode. So, you need to give space to allow for the other person to process what you have shared. In the case of unconscious bias, the other person is most likely not fully aware of their behavior. You may be the first person who has ever said this to them, so give them a little time for your words to sink it. The hope is that the other person uses that time not to mount a defense, but to think thoughtfully about what you said and ask for examples.

After the pause, and after the person has processed your approach, you can begin to share specific examples. But again, be careful to not go down a laundry list of past behavior.

Be succinct and specific. "I believe it's important that I be included on email strings that involve decisions on product development. Last week, I was not included on a key decision that directly affected our delivery schedule. As a result, I was not able to properly inform the marketing team on a release date." You have shared both your feelings, the conflict, and how it impacted you and the company. You have not made accusations of bias. You have left it open for the other person to react without feeling the need to be defensive. And you have allowed enough grace in your wording to allow the other person to "save face" and offer corrective action.

Also, stay open to the fact that you could have misperceived the situation. You do not have to be right and the other person wrong. That is not the objective of the conversation. Your objective is to try to resolve a perceived bias. That resolution can be mutually beneficial. In fact, that is the ideal. However, it doesn't always work out that way.

Keep calm

When the conversation did not go as planned, make sure to keep calm. You made the decision earlier that the situation was important enough to you to address. This usually means that the relationship with the other person is also important. So, leave the discussion amicably when possible. Remember we are talking about unconscious bias. With conscious bias, you may well have to end the relationship if the other person's behavior is damaging to you.

I will also add a word of caution that it may be less volatile to confront a person one-on-one. If you choose to confront a larger group, you run the risk of a mob mentality with a definite ingroup/outgroup bias directed at you. If your intention is a resolution to the conflict, this will not end well. If your intention is confrontation alone with no desire for reconciliation, then you can proceed. But we all know from the well-televised protests and counterprotests that shouting each other down is not an effective way to change someone's attitude. In some cases, you just need to walk away to protect yourself. Save the transformational conversation for one-on-one or smaller group interaction.

Target of unconscious bias

We spend a lot of time in unconscious bias training addressing how to become aware and change our own unconscious bias. But what if the unconscious bias is directed toward you? What if you are on the receiving end? Just as we devised plans in Chapter 4 to address our own unconscious biases, we should also plan how to handle unconscious bias when we are targets. Much of the time, we may be too shocked to react, and that is why it's good to have a pre-rehearsed script in our head. But even if we have an action plan in place, it's also good to step back and get some perspective before we go rushing headlong into a situation.

With unconscious bias, sometimes we start with smaller strikes at the armor. We are making chinks in a lifetime of assumptions, so this can take time. Our conversation may offer the awareness the other person needs to raise their actions to the level of consciousness. This may not change their behavior right away, but we have planted a seed. Perhaps when the person acts similarly in the future, they will recall what we said and hesitate a bit and maybe even alter their behavior.

However, there is always the possibility that the person will completely dismiss the conversation as ridiculous or an overreaction. That is on them and not you. Your job is to share your perception. You are not responsible for the other person's behavior or reaction. Try to remain respectful in the conversation. You can control your own behavior, but some people do not want to change. The downside is, of course, that what you had thought was unconscious bias was actually conscious bias. That is disheartening, but at least you know where you stand, and you can work to extricate yourself from the situation by finding a new job, transferring to another department, reporting the encounter to HR when appropriate, or ending the relationship.

When I was in graduate school in Clemson, South Carolina, I worked in the IT department of a textile mill in a nearby small town. Most of the other employees were local, and all were men. I enjoyed the work and appreciated my direct bosses, who were from Atlanta. However, the actual work environment was terrible. The gender bias was blatant. One particular "good old boy" would often tell sexist jokes deliberately in front of me, and then look at me for a reaction. He sat directly across from me, and we were separated by a partition. Many times, he would speak loudly, talking to no one in particular, but obviously intended that I hear him. One time he started out, "Well, I would tell you what women are good for, but that little lady on the other side might get mad." He then laughed uproariously, and some of the other men joined in.

Not too long after that occasion, my bosses took me out to lunch. They knew I was graduating that spring, and they wanted to offer me a full-time position at the mill. I told them there was no way I was going to work in that type of environment permanently. It had been okay for a short-term gig because I knew I was out of there as soon as I graduated. But I also told them that they had a serious HR problem at the mill. The next woman may not be as willing to go along, and they had a perfect environment for a sexual harassment suit.

I share this story for a couple of reasons. First of all, this was not unconscious bias. It was blatant, constant gender bias that manifested as sexual harassment. So, I would never have gone through the RISK model with the "good old boy." It would have been pointless, and it was not important to me to have a collegial relationship with the guy. However, I could have chosen to address the issue with my bosses. I know they would have made some changes if I had asked. But as I was a short-timer, I decided to ride out the clock.

But the situation also makes me wonder—why did my bosses, who knew about the behavior and heard it, not take action? It was a different time then—1994, so the answer I come to is that it wasn't just one individual—it was part of the company culture. They would have had to fire most of the male employees, and where were they going to find qualified candidates to fill the positions? This was in a town with one flashing light—not even a red light. They wouldn't be able to attract new talent with the current culture either. This was sort of a head-in-the-sand moment: if you don't have women in the workplace, there is no need to address the sexism and misogynistic comments. Obviously, that is a ridiculous way to run a company, but I don't think it's too far off from what goes on today when we refer to "locker room talk" or letting "boys be boys." But perhaps some of the men were uncomfortable with the talk but succumbed to group think. None of them ever spoke up in the six months I was working there.

The bottom line is the RISK model will help you decide how to deal with unconscious bias. For conscious bias, it is a whole lot more complicated, and it can be all-consuming.

Unconscious bias offender

But what if you are the unconscious bias offender? Perhaps someone confronts you about your behavior. That time will come because we all have unconscious biases by the fact that we are human. How do you react?

1. *Listen.* As we talked about in the previous section, our tendency is to rush in and defend ourselves or dismiss the allegations. But we need to tamp down that urge and listen respectfully to what the other person has to say, without interrupting. As we discussed in Chapter 5, this is listening generously, not thinking about what we are going to say next but focusing on the words and tone of the other person.

2. *Ask for an example.* Much of the time we will be so emotionally charged by allegations of unconscious bias that we don't get past the listening piece. But after we have listened thoughtfully, we should seek more information. That's the funny thing about unconscious bias—we are not aware of it, so examples help us to picture our own behavior and make it less likely we will dismiss the charges.

3. *Assume good intentions.* Just like in the RISK model, we should assume good intentions from the person making the assertion. Unless we know otherwise, the other person felt this situation was important enough to bring up to you, so it is not an effort to shame or belittle you.

4. *Do not respond defensively.* Focus on listening. And, for goodness' sake, if the situation is about race or gender, do not reply with any of the following:

   - I am the least racist person you will ever meet.

   - I have Black (Brown, LGBTQ+, disabled, etc.) friends or family members.

   - I dated an Asian (or Black, Hispanic, etc.) guy/girl.

   - I respect women.

   - I do not have a racist or misogynist bone in my body.

   These suggest the quote from Queen Gertrude in Hamlet, "The lady protests too much, methinks."

5. *Consider the charges.* Take a step back and consider what has been said to you. Have you heard similar allegations from others? Ask for other opinions: "Mary said I tend to take over projects, especially from the women on the team. Have you known me to do this?" This is difficult because it takes a lot of maturity and desire for growth. But if you want to change your behavior to be more inclusive, it's a necessary change. You can even ask those around you to help call you out when you slip. I do this a lot. I do not want to knowingly say something offensive.

I had to confront my own unconscious bias when it came to a particular treatment option for children with Hunter syndrome. I was dismissive of it because I didn't know a lot about it. A good friend gently pointed this out to me, and I chose to listen without anger or defensiveness. I knew he had good intentions, so I fought the urge to argue, and I considered the charge.

I had discounted the treatment based on my own availability bias. I was only considering the evidence I knew personally. I thanked him, and I began to seek more knowledge to counter my bias.

Don't demand someone educate you

I want to give a word of caution that there is a difference between asking someone to "call you out" and asking them to "educate" you. For example, it is not the responsibility of a Black person to school you on the ways you are being racist. There is plenty enough written for you to do your own homework.

And you do not have the right to indulge in Black or Brown trauma stories by asking others about their racist experiences. If someone wants to share their experiences with you, they will. If you want to learn more, pick up a book on the topic or read an article. See the list of resources in the next chapter of this book.

There is also a difference between having a transformational conversation and asking someone to divulge their discrimination stories with you. Discrimination is painful. For many, to relive that for someone else's information-seeking or knowledge is too much. We should not force or implore someone to share their stories. If someone wants to freely share their experience, that is their choice.

Transformational conversation is a two-way sharing experience, with both parties choosing to voluntarily share. It is not intended as a means of probing. The benefit also goes both ways. Transformational conversation is to be used in a particular setting when you are in a "sharing mode." However, it can also be used as a tool with friends and family, if both are willing to participate.

And transformational conversation is different than the outlined RISK model when you are confronting unconscious bias. With RISK, you are using your listening skills, much like in transformational conversation, but you are not expecting a back-and-forth sharing of unconscious bias experiences.

Anyone will applaud you for learning more about the discrimination others suffer. But there are enough blog posts, videos, articles, and books written about the topic that you do not need to assault strangers or acquaintances with questions. If you want to learn about a particular perspective, you can read about it.

With the input from others and your own research, you now have an opportunity to plan for change. Eventually, with deliberate thought and practice—spending time in System 2, you will begin to override your unconscious biases in System 1 with positive change.

When to withdraw

Sometimes no matter how well you have followed the RISK model or listened generously, you will run into a brick wall with unconscious bias. And continued conversation will only lead you to banging your head against that wall.

I have had the unpleasant experience twice of hearing from a surgeon who was identified as an expert in orthopedic issues in the mucopolysaccharidoses diseases or MPS at two different conferences I attended.

The first time I heard the surgeon speak, I was very interested. Boys with Hunter syndrome have serious issues with carpal tunnel syndrome because of the buildup of large sugar molecules called glycosaminoglycans (GAGs) in their joints. So, when he got to that part of his presentation, I perked my ears up. To my astonishment, the doctor said that carpal tunnel in our kids was painless. He had written "painless" in red and underlined it twice.

I knew from my own experiences with my son that this was wrong. Cole said, "Ow!" when I grabbed his hands before his carpal tunnel release surgery. After surgery, he took my hand willingly, even initiating it. And here was an "expert" telling a room full of people that carpal tunnel was painless. I felt my anger grow as he continued to emphasize this point. By the time he finished and opened for questions, I had walked myself through the RISK model, and I could barely stay in my seat. My hand shot up, and the microphone was brought to me. I took a breath and spoke, "You said in your presentation that carpal tunnel in kids with MPS was painless. How can you say that? I know my son with MPS II had excruciating pain to the point he could not tolerate having his hands even touched."

He gave a half-hearted answer about how in his experience none of his patients had expressed pain issues, but he then acknowledged as a surgeon that he didn't spend a great deal of time talking with patients. It was infuriating.

So, when the second incident occurred several months later, I was already primed. When he walked up to the podium to speak, I hoped he had made changes to his presentation based on the "feedback" I had given him at the last conference. I waited anxiously as he got to the part about carpal tunnel syndrome.

As he got to the slide, I saw it there again—"Painless"—in red and underlined twice. I could feel the heat start to rise in me. He had dismissed me. Here he was again, telling a room of two hundred plus people that carpal tunnel was painless in MPS. The arrogance of this so-called expert was too much. Again, when the question-and-answer period began, I raised my hand. As I stood up and started to speak, I heard him say, "Oh" and look down. I said, "Yes, I thought you might recognize me. As the parent of a child with MPS II who has had carpal tunnel release surgery, I strongly disagree with your statement that carpal tunnel is painless. My son had a great deal of pain before his surgery. So, on what evidence do you base that claim?"

He started to stammer and admitted that out of the forty patients he had seen, no one had complained of pain. But in the next breath he said a lot of them were non-verbal, so they couldn't express their pain. He was assuming because the kids could not express their pain through words that there was no pain.

I held back my anger and continued, "Well, that may be your experience, but we are all living with kids with MPS, and I can assure you that they let us know when they are in pain. I wouldn't want anyone listening to you to make the wrong decision about carpal tunnel surgery because they think carpal tunnel is painless." I was then encouraged that another doctor, an expert in the field of MPS diseases, stood after me to also disagree and correct the orthopedic doctor.

Having stood up twice in front of a large audience to challenge this same doctor, I still don't think he'll change his chart. Perhaps a one-on-one conversation would have been better? Maybe. But after talking to the organizers of the event, who had also spoken with him about that piece of his presentation, I don't think anything will penetrate his thinking. Instead, I will be there every time he speaks to our MPS II community to correct him. And as I write this and am currently helping to organize a conference for our community, I have asked a hand surgeon who is an expert on carpal tunnel in our boys to share directly with us. I consider this a direct rebuke to the misinformation promoted by a surgeon more concerned with his ego than his message.

Why unconscious bias training doesn't always work

We have talked now about why transformational conversations may not always work, but what about unconscious bias training generally? Does it work? It can, but too often the training is set up for failure. Some reasons for this failure include the following: (1) the training is too short; (2) there is no support from the top executives in the company; (3) the training is not interactive or experiential; 4) the training is not based on research, and the facilitators are untrained; or (5) the training is voluntary.

The training is too short.

Shortened unconscious bias training and video training are not going to be effective in creating change. In a one-hour training session, there is only time to concentrate on the first part of the process model—awareness or unfreeze. Dual-process theories in psychology also suggest any changes would be "highly contextual and short lived."[1,2,3,4] In addition, Joy-Gaba found in her research that a "shortened automatic bias education was not effective enough to significantly change participants' beliefs about bias and may not be a viable intervention to pursue."[5]

Having worked in a corporate environment for twenty years, I get it. Sometimes you are only given an hour for training. I was pushed into this trap of time myself. Ideally, I told the senior executives that the unconscious bias training session should span six hours. I was told that busy executives and salespeople could not afford to give up six hours for training. So, I condensed it down to four hours, eliminating a few exercises and tightening the time for individual reflection. Then, I was asked to take it to two hours and make it available online as a webinar. And finally, I was asked to create a forty-five-minute interactive video. I knew that educational research has shown that having others present helps facilitate learning[6] and leads to social comparisons.[7] My forty-five-minute video training session essentially translated to no real change.

One of the biggest reasons relates back to the perceived "lack of time" for diversity-related training. Putting aside only one hour out of the 2,080 hours in a typical work year signals a lack of commitment to diversity and the desire to only check a box for training.

There is no support from the top executives in the company.

In my experience, the time allocated for training usually comes from the top. This can be great, if you have a leader at the top willing to prioritize diversity training and even sponsor the effort. However, it can be detrimental if you have executives who feel that diversity training takes away from their employees making money.

The benefits of diversity in the workplace are well-known and widely researched—better innovation, broader reflection of customers' perspectives, higher financial returns, etc. Equally as well-known is the fact that unconscious biases can prevent the creation of an inclusive environment. In addition, we know that diversity initiatives supported by the top management have a higher chance for success. Achieving the business benefits of an inclusive, engaged team should be more than a side-initiative of the HR department.

Diversity should be an integrated part of your company's strategy, weaved throughout every aspect of your business. Diversity and inclusion must be pervasive and part of every conversation, every product, every service, and every encounter. And that's not just because it's the right thing to do. Unconscious bias has been shown to influence the behavior between a buyer and seller, with subtle racial clues preventing a successful interaction.[8] Research also shows that putting diversity and inclusion center stage will increase your company's financial success and significantly reduce the high operational cost of disgruntled employees.[9,10,11,12,13,14] Companies with inclusive cultures have employees that take fewer sick days and are more willing to achieve and contribute and help to promote the company to their networks.[15,16,17,18]

Integrating diversity as a key performance indicator at the highest level is a best practice. As the saying goes, "you can't manage what you can't measure."

The training is not interactive.

In addition, mass trainings with two hundred plus participants are not going to be effective if you don't have experiential learning built in. I have managed large-scale trainings and virtual events, but I always adhere to the idea of a workshop. I have small breakout groups of twenty-five or less and have additional facilitators to help. You need to be able to see your participants one-on-one and engage with them. Unconscious bias training should not be a passive experience. As I have talked about throughout this book, participants need a transformational experience through conversation either with one-on-one interaction or in a small group. This interaction allows participants to hear a different perspective.

The training is not based on research and the facilitators are untrained.

It is unfortunate that much of what is passing for unconscious bias training is not based on evidence-based research, and this could backfire for
well-meaning companies.

Having spent twenty years in the corporate world, I know how many
diversity programs work and you probably do, as well. Your HR diversity
strategy is built on whatever airport bestseller is trending at the time; unfortunately, little of what is trending is backed by research. Instead, it is based
on anecdotes and "what worked at my previous job." Time-strapped and
overworked much of the time, we buy the slick packaging and promises of
quick fixes.

When my former company asked me to research unconscious bias
many years ago, I began with a search online. At the time, there wasn't a
tremendous amount written about the topic. At least, that is what I thought.

The truth is that I was looking in the wrong place. The real research
was going on in academia, not in the workplace, and much of it was not
accessible through a simple search box. There are meta-analyses and rich
research on what does and does not work to change unconscious biases.
So, why aren't we implementing what the research says? It's not accessible
to everyone. The academic journals are many times off-limits to anyone
outside of the university or require expensive subscriptions. And even if you
do get access, you'll need to read through ten to fifteen pages of unfamiliar
academic speak to find the key findings of the research. You can see why
that airport book is a more popular choice for busy practitioners.

In a study conducted by the Academy of Management Learning &
Education on implicit bias, the authors found that more than half of the 178
articles reviewed by the authors did not follow any theoretical tradition. In
other words, the content, design, and facilitation of the training was not
based on any proven method.[19]

Part of the reason unconscious bias training is not based on evidence-based research is because we have unqualified facilitators leading

the sessions. This is a delicate training that can quickly escalate emotionally. If you have a person facilitating who has done a couple of hours of work searching on the Internet to cobble together a class, you will have a disaster. People know when you are faking it. And this is one area that should not be faked. I have never had a training go exactly as scripted. In my facilitating, I need the deep knowledge of the topic to bring someone back on task, dig a little deeper, question someone else's and my own assumptions, and be able to react to the moment without relying on limited information. Just as a novice actor cannot improvise in live theater as well as a seasoned actor, an unqualified facilitator cannot rely on superficial knowledge to carry them through a session, if they want to make real change.

In addition, a facilitator must have the ability to customize the training for the audience and use real examples from the specific industry, organization, or institution. With the topic of unconscious bias, you must be genuine with your intent. Stale examples and unrelatable stories will turn off your audience. You need to do your homework and really understand the challenges faced in your participants' environment.

Unconscious bias is not a program that you can take off the shelf and use once a year. It is also more than sending employees through a one-hour training class. If the desire for unconscious bias training is behavioral change, we must look to validated evidenced-based approaches both in psychology and in adult education.

The training is voluntary.

Deciding whether your training should be mandatory or voluntary can also influence your training.

If you make it voluntary, you will guarantee a class mostly made up of people who are wanting to change. You are effectively "preaching to the choir." The few that do attend voluntarily are usually committed to learning about their own unconscious biases and what they can do to help. But you won't reach everyone who could benefit from the class.

Believe it or not, men are not signing up in droves for diversity training. I can understand why some of these men are reluctant. As the majority or "ingroup," there is little incentive to change the status quo because everything is perfectly fine from their point of view. And they don't want to sit through a class where they think they will be shamed for being in the majority and blamed for all the world's ails. This isn't just conjecture. Both these points are backed by extensive research.

If you make it mandatory, you will get a larger audience, but you will have some who are resentful of having to attend. And I know the difference in the first five minutes of the workshop—arms crossed defensively across their chests, sitting back in their chairs, and defiantly determined not to participate.

And in a time where it seems no one wants to do what they are told or forced to do, this can completely backfire. Research has shown that mandatory and external legal pressure may lead employees to feel the pledge to diversity is being forced.[20,21]

So, should training be mandatory or voluntary? The research on this question is not conclusive, but some research suggests that mandatory may be better. The reasoning is that mandatory signals the companies have a firm commitment to inclusion. In addition, voluntary may not bring in the participants that would most benefit from the training.

It all comes down to knowing the employees, the culture, and the local environment. I have facilitated sessions that were voluntary and ones that were mandatory. I saw success with both, but only because I tailored my training to my audience. Mandatory has a definite place in diversity training, and I lean toward this approach. However, I would add a caveat that the training needs be well-designed, experiential, an effective length for change, and be followed with the appropriate reinforcement and nudges. I also definitely recommend you not call it diversity training. I try to tie it to leadership training whenever possible. Almost everyone wants to be a better leader or manager, and unconscious bias training can help with that.

Unconscious bias is present in every organization. And it's imperative for us to address it. But based on the current research on unconscious bias, behavioral change, and my own experience as a diversity leader conducting unconscious bias workshops, we as practitioners, leaders, and employers need to step back and look at what we are promoting to employees. We cannot expect to create effective education without considering our audience. So, let's sum it up:

1. *Diversity, Equity, and Inclusion education should not be punitive.* No one wants to be required to go to training because of his/her bad behavior. This is an unwilling audience. They will sit with their arms crossed and never hear the words you say. This type of training will ultimately backfire. But punitive is different from mandatory. If you make the training mandatory, everyone is required to attend, so individuals will not feel singled out.

2. *You cannot exclude 60 percent to 70 percent of your audience.* As we said in the last chapter, unconscious bias training cannot be a finger pointing occasion. In North America, White males are still the majority in leadership positions. The education session must be developed with this key audience in mind. If we want change, we need the help of the "ingroup." We cannot alienate those that hold power and make decisions. With diversity must also come inclusion. We need these men as allies, not adversaries.

3. *Change will not come overnight.* For those companies thinking that they can hold a forty-five-minute training and then have an inclusive environment, it's not going to happen. Unconscious biases are built over time and almost hard-wired into our brains. A short session shaming and accusing employees will also not work. There needs to be an investment in both time and support from the leadership team to see real change.

4. *Classes should be experiential.* Mass training or video training without some element of interaction or a facilitator-led discussion

will not work because you are creating a passive experience that allows participants to easily fade into the crowd, tune-out, or not participate. I make sure everyone is engaged in the workshop and actively participating.

Taking these points into consideration, you can begin to focus on what works to create change in unconscious bias. But even as we have talked about ways to create a successful unconscious bias training and use transformational conversation, you should know there is no silver bullet. Unconscious biases have developed over time, so time must be part of the solution. But we want to make sure we use time as a tool, not as a substitute for complacency. As Martin Luther King, Jr. so wisely said:

> Actually, time itself is neutral; it can be used either destructively or constructively. More and more I feel that the people of ill will have used time much more effectively than have the people of good will. We will have to repent in this generation not merely for the hateful words and actions of the bad people but for the appalling silence of the good people. Human progress never rolls in on wheels of inevitability; it comes through the tireless efforts of men willing to work to be co-workers with God, and without this hard work, time itself becomes an ally of the forces of social stagnation. We must use time creatively, in the knowledge that the time is always ripe to do right.[22]

With the words of MLK in mind, I challenge you to seize the moment, examine your own unconscious biases, and vow to make changes. Plan now and follow through with it.

Unconscious bias training isn't a free pass

Lastly, someone recently sent me an article from the Huffington Post criticizing unconscious bias training as letting "white people" off the hook for their biases. The author reasoned that by telling people that their biases were unconscious, we were giving them an "out"—a way to separate themselves from the guilt or stigma associated with biases.

As a facilitator and researcher of unconscious bias, I find this line of reasoning faulty. I stress during my unconscious bias workshops that everyone has bias. But I also challenge all participants. In fact, I hold them accountable because they have gone through my training. I tell participants that now that they are aware that they have these biases, it is their responsibility to work to mitigate them. I intentionally call my sessions workshops because I believe it's only through working through our biases that we can attain change. And that is the goal of any unconscious bias training I do—change.

No one wants a finger pointed at them and to be told they are the problem. But most, when presented with the data, are willing allies and ambassadors for change because they understand the benefits and the positive role that they can play in building inclusive teams rather than supporting an "us" and "them" mentality.

In the next and last chapter, I will share with you resources to become a better ally, advocate, and promoter of change.

Chapter takeaways

- It's important to recognize when conversation alone is not going to change someone's unconscious or conscious bias. In those instances, you need to walk away.

- Use the RISK model of response when deciding what action to take. Risk: What are the risks to me if I respond? Important: Is it important for me to respond? Stay open: Stay open to the other person's perspective. Keep calm: If it does not go well, keep calm.

- When confronted with your own unconscious bias, I would suggest the following: (1) Listen, (2) Ask for an example, (3) Assume good intentions, (4) Do not respond defensively, and (5) Consider the charges.

- There are several reasons unconscious bias training may not be successful: (1) The training is too short; (2) There is no support from the top of the company or organization; (3) The training is not interactive, experiential, or does not invoke change; (4) The training is not based on research, and the facilitator does not know the material; and/or (5) The training is voluntary.

- To have a successful unconscious bias training, I would suggest the following: (1) Don't make it be punitive, (2) Don't exclude or shame potential audience members when designing the training, (3) Do invest in change beyond the training, and (4) Do make your training experiential.

CHAPTER 7.

CONCLUSION

Goal: Provide resources for the reader to continue their journey with unconscious bias.

My Dad was admitted to the hospital several years ago for unexplained symptoms: he was extremely tired, felt very weak, and he couldn't seem to catch his breath. For several days, the hospital staff was baffled about what was wrong with my dad. They were treating him with antibiotics, but he was not improving. Finally, someone contacted an infectious disease doctor, and he drew a blood sample from the site of my dad's port-a-catheter, which he had placed for his cancer treatment years ago. With that background, I'll pick up the dialogue that ensued between the doctor, my dad, and me.

Doctor: "You see, Mr. Stephens sometimes we have bacteria that enters our body through an outside source. If that bacterium gets into our bloodstream, then it can cause harm. When you have a port-a-cath, you have a direct line into your heart, and bacteria can be introduced in a variety of ways . . ."

He went on like this for a while, and my dad was starting to get very anxious and was looking at me like, "What the hell is this guy talking about?"

Me: "So, what you are saying is that he has a port infection, and his port-a-cath needs to come out?"

The doctor ignores me and continues to look at Dad.

Doctor: "In these cases, we need to treat the source of the infection."

My dad is visibility agitated, and he points to me.

Dad: "She knows a lot about these types of things."

The doctor smiles condescendingly at my dad.

Doctor: "Oh? She picked a thing or two up at the barbershop?"

I fight back the urge to say something sarcastically and instead reply confidently.

Me: "No, my four-year-old son had a port infection and had to have aortic-valve replacement surgery because the strep bacteria ate through his valve. So, I do have some experience with this type of thing."

Doctor:" Oh, . . ." (then silence).

This is a classic example of stereotyping and socioeconomic bias—the doctor made some assumptions—I could not be well-educated because my father was a barber. There was also some gender bias, as well. What could I know as a woman?

To address the situation, I had to take a deep breath and think about what would be helpful in this situation. I could see my dad was getting anxious the more the doctor talked to him. The doctor wasn't being clear, and my dad was looking for the bottom line. In this case, I had the advantage of knowing my father well, so I knew he needed a quick synopsis and then the details could come after. I put aside my anger and focused on reassuring my dad that once his port was out, he would get better and be able to leave the hospital. I explained that the port was like a condominium complex for bacteria. They love it and invite their friends to move in. One of my son's neurosurgeons had explained this to me, so it wasn't knowledge I had picked up at the barbershop. But even if it was, what was the doctor's point of being condescending and implying that no useful knowledge is picked up at the barbershop?

I include this as my final story of the book because it illustrates how unconscious bias can show up at any time and anywhere. We must be vigilant to see it and respond. In this case with the doctor, my father and I were very aware of the socioeconomic and less-educated stereotype associated with him being a barber. We have dealt with it most of our lives. Because of this experience, I was able to respond to the doctor, and I chose to do it. Now that you have the knowledge and tools, I hope you will make your own choice on when and how to respond or not.

Future research

In writing this book, I focused narrowly on unconscious bias in the typical workplace. I wanted you to be able to pick up this book and read it in one to two sessions. My intent was for you to be able to begin implementing the principles right away, so you can see change. But in doing so, I also limited the scope of the impact of unconscious bias.

There are so many opportunities for future research on unconscious bias. We need more longitudinal studies to understand the staying power of unconscious bias training. How do we employ cognitive nudges in the moment to reinforce the learnings?

I also did not dive deep enough into gender and racial bias. Both are inherent in all the biases we talked about. But I think they both warrant their own exploration in future books. In addition, there is a lot written that we can learn from. That is why I devoted this chapter to resources I recommend and have personally read with the hope you will continue your learning.

These books also give you the opportunity to view unconscious and conscious bias from different perspectives—a key tenet of this book. I offer my own cisgender, white, female perspective, so I encourage you to seek out other voices and learn. As I have said many times, it is your responsibility to educate yourself and work to be more inclusive.

In addition to the substantial list of resources in the notes section at the end of this book, I invite you to continue your journey with unconscious bias with the following books:

Books on unconscious bias/cognitive biases

- *Biased: Uncovering the Hidden Prejudice that Shapes What we See, Think, and Do* by Jennifer Eberhardt

- *Thinking Fast and Slow* by Daniel Kahneman

- *Blindspot* by Mahzarin Banaji and Anthony Greenwald

- *Everyday Bias* by Howard J. Ross

- *Overcoming Bias* by Tiffany Jana and Matthew Freeman

- *Creative Change* by Jennifer Mueller

- *Blink* by Malcolm Gladwell

So many times, I had to pause my writing to react to current events: the January 6 riot, Ahmaud Arbery's modern-day lynching, the shooting of Breonna Taylor, George Floyd's murder, and so many more. As with many other diversity, equity, and inclusion consultants, my phone ringing seemed to be synchronized with the news cycle. The calls for workshops peaked when outrage was high and then would settle back down again with the next news cycle. I had to make deliberate decisions to not address these events in this book and stay focused on unconscious bias and not conscious bias. My voice is not the one that needs to be heard on these topics. Instead, I will highlight and magnify Black and Brown voices.

Books about racial bias

- *Caste* by Isabel Wilkerson

- *Why Are All the Black kids Sitting Together in the Cafeteria?* by Beverly Daniel Tatum

- *Can We Talk about Race? And Other Conversations in an Era of School Resegregation* by Beverly Daniel Tatum
- *Medical Apartheid* by Harriet A. Washington
- *Stamped from the Beginning* by Ibram X. Kendi
- *How to be an Antiracist* by Ibram X. Kendi

Books dealing with gender

- *The Essential Difference: The Truth about the Male and Female Brain* by Simon Baron-Cohen
- *Why Women: The Leadership Imperative to Advancing Women and Engaging Men* by Jeffery Tobias Halter
- *What Works: Gender Equality by Design* by Iris Bohnet
- *That's What She Said: What Men Need to Know (And Women Need to Tell Them) About Working Together* by Joanne Lipman
- *Difference Matters: Communicating Social Identity, Second Edition* by Brenda J. Allen

Books on conversation

- *We Need to Talk* by Celeste Headlee
- *Race Dialogues: A Facilitator's Guide to Tackling the Elephant in the Classroom* by Donna Rich Kaplowitz, Shayla Reese Griffin, and Sheri Seyka
- *So You Want to Talk About Race* by Ijeoma Oluo
- *Building Relationships One Conversation at a Time* by Carol Ann Lloyd-Stanger

Books on diversity, equity, and inclusion

- *Inclusion: Diversity, the New Workplace & the Will to Change* by Jennifer Brown

- *The Difference: How the Power of Diversity Creates Better Groups, Firms, Schools, and Societies* by Scott E. Page

- *The Diversity Bonus* by Scott E. Page

- *Latino Talent: Effective Strategies to Recruit, Retain, and Develop Hispanic Professionals* by Robert Rodriguez

- *The End of Diversity as We Know It* by Martin Davidson

- *Inclusion Nudges* by Lisa Kepinski and Tinna C. Nielsen

- *Nudge: Improving Decisions About Health, Wealth, and Happiness* by Richard H. Thaler and Cass R. Sunstein

I also recommend *Diversity Managers: Angels of Mercy or Barbarians at the Gate* by Shelton J. Goode for a comprehensive list of other recommended books on DEI.

You can refer to my website InclusiveThinking.org for more information, blog posts, and resources.

ACKNOWLEDGEMENTS

My work on this book started initially back in 2015, when I chose to focus on implicit bias for my dissertation. But the initial thinking of the topic goes back to when the chief diversity officer at the time at IBM, Belinda Tang, handed me a book, *Blind Spot*, and asked me to figure out this "unconscious bias" thing for the company. I thank her for trusting me to take on such an immense task. I owe many at IBM for their help and mentoring over the years: Shannon Rapuano, Andi Snow-Weaver, Chuck King, Sara Basson, Paula Kwit, Heather Howell, Ron Glover, Ana Martinez, Joan Mockler, Mark Harris, Ed Barbini, Shari Chiara, and Mike Maney. All have been relentless champions for me. I would like to thank all those who have encouraged me over the years as I started my own journey exploring unconscious bias. If you have read any of my blog posts, responded to my postings, attended a workshop, or listened as I shared my thoughts, you are part of this book. Thank you to all my clients who have trusted me to guide you through creating inclusive workplaces. I have learned so much from these encounters and experiences. And to all my family and friends who have indulged my "blue-sky" thinking, I appreciate you cheering me on through my goals and dreams.

I would like to thank my doctoral advisor, Richard Baskerville, for patiently pushing me to dig deeper and embrace theory. He forced me to stay in System 2 thinking when I often wanted to retreat to the more comfortable System 1.

I owe a great debt to Lars Mathiassen for his constant encouragement and not very subtle reminders to finish the book. His advice and guidance influenced every page.

In addition, I give a great deal of credit and thanks to my fellow Georgia State alumni and professors. I don't believe I would have reached this milestone without the knowledge I gained from each of you. Pam Ellen, Karen Loch, Arun Rai, and Todd Mauer, I appreciate the many hours you spent teaching me to be a better researcher. I especially want to call out the influence of my "after hours" conversations with Kofi Smith, Ginger Lange, Alvin Glay, Veneetia Johnson, Deborah Hazzard, and Jorge Vallejos. Equally as important are the lively discussions I had with my GSU cohort: David Talley, Sheila Cappel, Kevin Morgan, Tony Annan, Al Tilooby, Derrick Warren, Kat Spradley, Melissa Furman, Ryan Bhattacharyya, and Carey Dukes.

On a personal level, it is hard to find the words to thank Sarah Lucchesi Napier. She stuck with me throughout the dissertation and this book and gave me the space to write. She has become like a daughter to me, and I will forever be grateful for her encouragement and love.

My sons, Cole and Connor, have molded who I am more than any humans. Cole is the bravest kid, and he reminds me every day to laugh and find joy in the little things. Connor has challenged me in ways I didn't know were possible, but he has also made me think about how I show up as a parent and model inclusion. I appreciate that not every teenager has conversations with their mom about unconscious and conscious bias. Bless him for listening patiently, engaging, and asking the hard questions.

Thank you to Jeff Mausolf for showing me and our children what amicability can look like when you put your children first.

My sister, Paula Buckingham, has always been my fiercest supporter and defender. I would not be who I am without her. She never hesitates to tell me how proud she is of me and to offer a restrained hug, with pats included.

I must give credit to my parents for raising me to always show kindness and help wherever I can. My mom always made sure everyone had a ride to the swim meets and took every kid who missed their bus stop home. She showed me with her actions what it meant to be an anti-racist and inclusive.

My grandmothers were my first role models. I never heard my Mamo Stephens say an unkind word about anyone. I strive to be the woman she believed I could be. She often told me she was "always a little foolish about me." My Mamo Rasar showed me that a strong woman isn't afraid to sweat and get her hands dirty. I can still remember how her rough, blackberry-stained hands felt. I am lucky to have aunts who continue modeling compassion and remind me of the strength of womanhood, coupled with empathy and love.

My MPS Dragon Moms have surrounded me with love and lifted me when I could have easily fallen. We are bonded in a way that few will understand, and I'm so grateful to walk alongside each of you. Thank you to Deb Cehak, Jamie Brooks, and Jen Carter for your immense wisdom and guidance. I hope we always have the courage to light the firecracker when we need to.

To the larger Hunter syndrome community, I am blessed to be a part of the "club that no one wants to be in." You all inspire me every day to get up and keep pushing for better treatments and a cure for our boys.

I would be remiss if I didn't acknowledge my best friend since childhood, Rhonda Jamease Kowalczyk, who most likely started me on this journey of conversation. Her friendship is so treasured that I'm reluctant to put words around it. She started me early talking about race and racism, and she is still that friend that challenges me when I need it.

Thank you to Cheryl Middleton for finding me when I was lost in a sea of red and sharing your experiences. Your strength and grace are inspirational.

To Karen Beatty, thank you for listening and pushing me up the hill.

My Phi Mu sisters, I have felt your cheers and your encouragement. I appreciate that you have always allowed me to be myself. I am blessed to have such strong women uplifting me. I will forever remember my sister Whit saying, "You are putting so much good back into the world." This is the highest compliment I could have received. LIOB, sisters.

I have to give a shoutout to my furry friends Lucy and Rosie. They allowed me to hug them and hold their paws on those tough days.

To my dear friend Angela Insenga, I save the last words. We have gone through the worst of storms and emerged stronger. Your brilliance inspires me to work harder and become the best form of myself. You were one of the first to give me the courage to have tough conversations and show me how to listen generously. Who would have thought we would be where we are today when scraping together our dollars for a visit to Backstreets?

NOTES AND REFERENCES

Chapter 1

1. Ross, H. J. (2014). *Everyday Bias: Identifying and Navigating Unconscious Judgments in Our Daily Lives.* Rowman & Littlefield.

2. Kahneman, D. (2011). *Thinking, Fast and Slow.* Macmillan, pp. 29–30.

3. Kahneman, D. (2011). *Thinking, Fast and Slow.* Macmillan, p. 20.

4. Kahneman, D. (2011). *Thinking, Fast and Slow.* Macmillan, p. 21.

5. McConnell, A. R., & Leibold, J. M. (2001). *Relations among the Implicit Association Test, discriminatory behavior, and explicit measures of racial attitudes. Journal of experimental social psychology, 37*(5), 435–442.

6. Bertrand, M., & Mullainathan, S. (2004). *Are Emily and Greg more employable than Lakisha and Jamal? A field experiment on labor market discrimination. American economic review, 94*(4), 991-1013.

7. Legault, L., Green-Demers, I., & Eadie, A. L. (2009). *When internalization leads to automatization: The role of self-determination in automatic stereotype suppression and implicit prejudice regulation. Motivation and Emotion, 33*(1), 10–24.

8. Devine, P. G., Forscher, P. S., Austin, A. J., & Cox, W. T. (2012). *Long-term reduction in implicit race bias: A prejudice habit-breaking*

intervention. *Journal of experimental social psychology*, 48(6), 1267–1278.

9. Burnes, B. (2007). *Kurt Lewin and the Harwood studies: The foundations of OD. The Journal of Applied Behavioral Science*, 43(2), 229.

10. Burnes, B. (2004). *Kurt Lewin and the planned approach to change: a re-appraisal. Journal of Management studies*, 41(6), 977–1002.

11. Stephens, K., (2018*). Managing implicit bias with transformational conversation: A qualitative field study of social identity theory.* https:// scholarworks.gsu.edu/bus_admin_diss/97.

Chapter 2

1. Banaji, M. R. & Greenwald, A. G. (2013). *Blindspot: Hidden Biases of Good People.* First edition. Delacorte Press.

2. Cognitive Bias Codex. Available at https://www.visualcapitalist. com/wp-content/uploads/2021/08/all-188-cognitive-biases.html.

3. Levine, M., Prosser, A., Evans, D., & Reicher, S. (2005*). Identity and emergency intervention: How social group membership and inclusiveness of group boundaries shape helping behavior. Personality and Social Psychology Bulletin, 31*(4), 443–453. https://doi. org/10.1177/0146167204271651.

4. Levine, M., Prosser, A., Evans, D., & Reicher, S. (2005). *Identity and emergency intervention: How social group membership and inclusiveness of group boundaries shape helping behavior. Personality and Social Psychology Bulletin, 31*(4), 443–453. https://doi. org/10.1177/0146167204271651.

5. Anthony, S. D. (2016). *Kodak's downfall wasn't about technology. Harvard Business Review.* https://hbr.org/2016/07/ kodaks-downfall-wasnt-about-technology.

6. Devine, P. G., Forscher, P. S., Austin, A. J., & Cox, W. T. (2012). *Long-term reduction in implicit race bias: A prejudice habit-breaking*

intervention. Journal of experimental social psychology, 48(6), 1267–1278.

7. Bargh, J. A. (1999). *The cognitive monster: The case against the controllability of automatic stereotype effects.* In S. Chaiken & Y. Trope (Eds.), *Dual-Process Theories in Social Psychology.* pp. 361–382. The Guilford Press.

8. Devine, P. G. (1989*). Stereotypes and prejudice: Their automatic and controlled components. Journal of personality and social psychology, 56* (1), 5.

9. Dovidio, J. F., & Gaertner, S. L. (1986). *Prejudice, Discrimination, and Racism. Academic Press.*

10. Banaji, M. R., Bhaskar, R., & Brownstein, M. (2015). *When bias is implicit, how might we think about repairing harm? Current Opinion in Psychology,* 6, 184.

Chapter 3

1. Gaucher, D., Friesen, J., & Kay, A. C. (2011). *Evidence that gendered wording in job advertisements exists and sustains gender inequality. Journal of personality and social psychology, 101*(1), 109.

2. See the context for structured interviews: Kahneman, D. (2011). *Thinking Fast and Slow,* p. 232.

Chapter 4

1. Maya Angelou, (2018, August 12). *Twitter.*

2. Newman, M. (2020, August 13). *Dolly Parton steers her empire through the pandemic—and keeps it growing. Billboard* magazine, https://www.billboard.com/music/country/dolly-parton-country-power-players-billboard-cover-story-interview-2020-9432581/.

3. Allport, G. W. (1954). *The Nature of Prejudice*. Cambridge, MA: Perseus Books.

4. Devine, P. G., Forscher, P. S., Austin, A. J., & Cox, W. T. (2012). *Long-term reduction in implicit race bias: A prejudice habit-breaking intervention. Journal of Experimental Social Psychology*, 48(6), 1267-1278.

5. Conversation. (n.d.) In *Cambridge Academic Content Dictionary*. Retrieved from https://dictionary.cambridge.org/us/dictionary/english/conversation.

6. Baron-Cohen, S. (2003). *The Essential Difference: The Truth about the Male & Female Brain*. Basic Books.

7. Burnes, B. (2007). *Kurt Lewin and the Harwood studies: The foundations of OD. The Journal of Applied Behavioral Science*, 43(2), 229.

8. Gilbert, D.T., Fiske, S. T., Lindzey, G. (1998). *The Handbook of Social Psychology*, Vol. 2. New York: McGraw-Hill Hirsch and Cha, 2017.

9. Forscher, P. S. L., Calvin, K.; Axt, J. R.; Ebersole, C. R.; Herman, M., Devine, P.G., & Nosek, B. A. (2017). *A Meta-Analysis of Change in Implicit Bias*. Unpublished.

10. Linnehan, F., Konrad, A. M., Reitman, F., Greenhalgh, A., & London, M. (2003). *Behavioral goals for a diverse organization: The effects of attitudes, social norms, and racial identity for Asian Americans and Whites. Journal of Applied Social Psychology*, 33(7), 1331-1359.

11. Ross, H. J. (2014). *Everyday Bias: Identifying and Navigating Unconscious Judgments in Our Daily Lives*. Rowman & Littlefield.

12. Dover, T., Major, B., & Kaiser, C. (2016). *Diversity policies rarely make companies fairer, and they feel threatening to white men. Harvard Business Review*, 1–6.

13. Von Bergen, C.W., Soper, B., & Foster, T. (2002). *Unintended negative effects of diversity management. Public Personnel Management, 31,* 239–25.

14. Jackson, S.E., & Joshi, A. (2010). Work team diversity. In S. Zedeck (ed.), *APA Handbook of Industrial and Organizational Psychology,* Volume 1, pp. 651–686.

15. Kalev, A., Dobbin, F., & Kelly, E. (2006). *Best practices or best guesses? Assessing the efficacy of corporate affirmative action and diversity policies. American sociological review, 71*(4), 589-617.

16. Joy-Gaba, J. (2011). *From Learning to Doing: The Effects of Educating Individuals on the Pervasiveness of Bias* (Doctoral dissertation). Retrieved from https://doi.org/10.18130/V3W804.

17. Senge, P. M. (1994). *The Fifth Discipline Fieldbook: Strategies and Tools for Building a Learning Organization.* New York: Currency, Doubleday. The ladder of inference was first developed by Chris Argyris.

18. Devine, P.G. (1989). *Stereotypes and prejudice: Their automatic and controlled components. Journal of personality and social psychology, 56* (1), 5.

19. Devine, P. G., Forscher, P. S., Austin, A. J., & Cox, W. T. (2012). *Long-term reduction in implicit race bias: A prejudice habit-breaking intervention. Journal of Experimental Social Psychology, 48*(6), 1267-1278.

20. Senge, P. M. (1994). *The Fifth Discipline Fieldbook: Strategies and Tools for Building a Learning Organization.* New York: Currency, Doubleday. The ladder of inference was first developed by Chris Argyris.

21. Devine, P.G. (1989). *Stereotypes and prejudice: Their automatic and controlled components. Journal of Personality and Social Psychology, 56* (1), 5.

22. Devine, P. G., Forscher, P. S., Austin, A. J., & Cox, W. T. (2012). *Long-term reduction in implicit race bias: A prejudice habit-breaking intervention. Journal of Experimental Social Psychology, 48*(6), 1267–1278.

23. Joy-Gaba, J. (2011). *From Learning to Doing: The Effects of Educating Individuals on the Pervasiveness of Bias* (Doctoral dissertation). Retrieved from https://doi.org/10.18130/V3W804.

24. Eberhardt, J. (2019). *Biased: Uncovering the Hidden Prejudice that Shapes What We See, Think, and Do.* New York: Viking, p. 35.

25. Burnes, B. (2004). *Kurt Lewin and the planned approach to change: A re-appraisal. Journal of Management Studies,* 41: 977–1002.

26. Gollwitzer, P. M., Sheeran, P., Trötschel, R., & Webb, T. L. (2011). *Self-regulation of priming effects on behavior. Psychological Science, 22*(7), 901–907.

27. St Quinton, T., & Brunton, J. A. (2017). *Implicit processes, self-regulation, and interventions for behavior change. Frontiers in Psychology, 8,* 346.

28. Stewart, B. D., & Payne, B. K. (2008). *Bringing automatic stereotyping under control: Implementation intentions as efficient means of thought control. Personality and Social Psychology Bulletin, 34*(10), 1332–1345.

29. Correll, J., Park, B., Judd, C. M., & Wittenbrink, B. (2002). *The police officer's dilemma: Using ethnicity to disambiguate potentially threatening individuals. Journal of Personality and Social Psychology, 83*(6), 1314.

30. Mendoza, S. A., Gollwitzer, P. M., & Amodio, D. M. (2010). *Reducing the expression of implicit stereotypes: Reflexive control through implementation intentions. Personality and Social Psychology Bulletin, 36*(4), 512–523.

31. Eberhardt, J. (2019). *Biased: Uncovering the Hidden Prejudice that Shapes What We See, Think, and Do.* New York: Viking.

32. Apfelbaum, E. P., Pauker, K., Sommers, S. R., & Ambady, N. (2010*). In blind pursuit of racial equality? Psychological Science, 21*(11), 1587–1592.

33. Eberhardt, J. (2019). *Biased: Uncovering the Hidden Prejudice that Shapes What We See, Think, and Do.* New York: Viking, p. 217.

34. Kahneman, D. (2011*). Thinking, Fast and Slow.* Macmillan.

35. Lindsey, A., King, E., Hebl, M., & Levine, N. (2015). *The impact of method, motivation, and empathy on diversity training effectiveness. Journal Of Business and Psychology,* 30(3), 605-617. p. 614).

36. Wilkerson, I. (2020). *Caste: The Origins of Our Discontents.* New York, Random House. p. 373.

37. Wilkerson, I. (2020). *Caste: The Origins of Our Discontents.* New York, Random House. p. 373.

Chapter 5

1. Gaucher, D., Friesen, J., & Kay, A. C. (2011). *Evidence that gendered wording in job advertisements exists and sustains gender inequality. Journal of Personality and Social Psychology,* 101(1), 109.

2. Gender Decoder. Available at http://gender-decoder.katmatfield. com.

3. Carroll, J. B. (ed.) (1997) [1956]. *Language, Thought, and Reality: Selected Writings of Benjamin Lee Whorf.* Cambridge, Mass.: Technology Press of Massachusetts Institute of Technology.

4. Eberhardt, J. L., Dasgupta, N., & Banaszynski, T. L. (2003). *Believing is seeing: The effects of racial labels and implicit beliefs on face perception. Personality and Social Psychology Bulletin,* 29, 360–370.

5. Darley, J.M., Gross, P.H. (1983). *A hypothesis-confirming bias in labeling effects. Journal of Personality and Social Psychology, 44*, 20–33.

6. Challa, J. (2013, December 30). *Why being 'gypped' hurts the Roma more than it hurts you. NPR: Code Switch.* www.npr.org/sections/codeswitch/2013/12/30/242429836/why-being-gypped-hurts-the-roma-more-than-it-hurts-you.

7. Tiffany Crutcher, sister of Terence Crutcher who was shot by Tulsa police, talks at a press conference. *Tulsa World.* Archived from the original on September 26, 2016.

8. Ross, H. J. (2014). *Everyday Bias: Identifying and Navigating Unconscious Judgments in Our Daily Lives.* Rowman & Littlefield.

9. Ross, H. J. (2014). *Everyday Bias: Identifying and Navigating Unconscious Judgments in Our Daily Lives.* Rowman & Littlefield.

10. Harquail, C. V., & Cox, T. (1993). *Organizational culture and acculturation. Cultural Diversity in Organizations, 161*, 176.

11. Linnehan, F., Konrad, A. M., Reitman, F., Greenhalgh, A., & London, M. (2003). *Behavioral goals for a diverse organization: The effects of attitudes, social norms, and racial identity for Asian Americans and Whites. Journal of Applied Social Psychology, 33*(7), 1332.

12. Bobo, L., & Kluegel, J. R. (1993). *Opposition to race-targeting: self-interest, stratification ideology, or racial attitudes? American Sociological Review*, 443-464.

13. Tougas, F., & Beaton, A. M. (1993). *Affirmative action in the work place: For better or for worse. Applied Psychology: An International Review.*

14. Messner, M. A. (1998). *The Limits of "The Male Sex Role" An Analysis of the Men's Liberation and Men's Rights Movements' Discourse. Gender & Society, 12*(3), 255–276.

15. Jacques, R. (1997). *The Unbearable Whiteness of Being. Managing the Organizational Melting Pot: Dilemmas of Workplace Diversity.* Thousand Oaks, CA.

16. Linnehan, F., Konrad, A. M., Reitman, F., Greenhalgh, A., & London, M. (2003). *Behavioral goals for a diverse organization: The effects of attitudes, social norms, and racial identity for Asian Americans and Whites. Journal of Applied Social Psychology, 33*(7), 1337.

17. Ross, H. J. (2014). *Everyday Bias: Identifying and Navigating Unconscious Judgments in Our Daily Lives.* Rowman & Littlefield, p. 118.

18. Ross, H. J. (2014). *Everyday Bias: Identifying and Navigating Unconscious Judgments in Our Daily Lives.* Rowman & Littlefield, p. 109.

19. Joy-Gaba, J. (2011). *From Learning to Doing: The Effects of Educating Individuals on the Pervasiveness of Bias* (Doctoral dissertation). Retrieved from https://doi.org/10.18130/V3W804, p. 111.

Chapter 6

1. Epstein, S. (1994). *Integration of the cognitive and the psychodynamic unconscious. American Psychologist, 49*(8), 709.

2. Smith, E. R., & DeCoster, J. (2000). *Dual-process models in social and cognitive psychology: Conceptual integration and links to underlying memory systems. Personality and Social Psychology Review, 4*(2), 108–131.

3. Strack, F., & Deutsch, R. (2004). *Reflective and impulsive determinants of social behavior. Personality and Social Psychology Review, 8*(3), 220–247.

4. Devine, P. G., Forscher, P. S., Austin, A. J., & Cox, W. T. (2012). *Long-term reduction in implicit race bias: A prejudice habit-breaking*

intervention. Journal of Experimental Social Psychology, 48(6), 1267–1278.

5. Joy-Gaba, J. (2011). *From Learning to Doing: The Effects of Educating Individuals on the Pervasiveness of Bias* (Doctoral dissertation). Retrieved from https://doi.org/10.18130/V3W804, p. 105.

6. Doise, W., Mugny, G., James, A. S., Emler, N., & Mackie, D. (2013). *The social development of the intellect.* (Vol. 10). Elsevier.

7. Kruglanski, A. W., & Mayseless, O. (1990). *Classic and current social comparison research: Expanding the perspective. Psychological bulletin, 108*(2), 195.

8. Stephens, K., & Baskerville, R. L. (2020). *The impact of implicit bias on business-to-business marketing. Journal of Business & Industrial Marketing.* https://doi.org/10.1108/JBIM-01-2019-0019.

9. Catalyst. (2002). *Making Change: Creating a business case for diversity.*

10. Carter, N. M. & Wagner, H.M. (2011). *The bottom line: Corporate performance and women's representation on boards* (2004–2008). Catalyst.

11. Dezso, C. & Ross, D. (2008, June 13). *When women rank high, firms profit. Columbia Business School Ideas at Work.*

12. Ozanian, M. K. (2010, October 25). *Girls rule. Forbes.*

13. Herring, C. (2009, April). *Does diversity pay?: Race, gender, and the business case for diversity. American Sociological Review, 74,*(2).

14. Avery, D. R., McKay, P. F., Tonidandel, S., Volpone, S. D., & Morris, M. A. (Spring 2012). *Is there method to the madness? Examining how racioethnic matching influences retail store productivity. Personnel Psychology, 65.*

15. Kaplan, D. M., Wiley, J. W., & Maertz Jr., C. P. (2011). *The role of calculative attachment in the relationship between diversity climate and retention. Human Resource Management, 50,*(2).

16. McKay, P. F., Avery, D. R., Tonidandel, S., Morris, M. A., Hernandez, M., & Hebl, M. R. (Spring 2007). *Racial differences in employee retention: Are diversity climate perceptions the key? Personnel Psychology, 60*,(1).

17. *Attention to diversity pays off: A conversation with Murat Philippe.* (2007). *HR Solutions International, Inc.*

18. *Driving performance and retention through employee engagement.* (2004). Corporate Leadership Council, Washington, DC.

19. Bezrukova, K., Jehn, K. A., & Spell, C. S. (2012). *Reviewing diversity training: Where we have been and where we should go. Academy of Management Learning & Education,* 11(2), 207–227.

20. Legault, L., Green-Demers, I., & Eadie, A. L. (2009). *When internalization leads to automatization: The role of self-determination in automatic stereotype suppression and implicit prejudice regulation. Motivation and Emotion, 33*(1), 10–24.

21. Dobbin, F., & Kalev, A. (2018). *Why doesn't diversity training work? The challenge for industry and academia. Anthropology Now, 10*(2), 48–55.

22. King, M.L., (1963). *Why We Can't Wait: Letter from Birmingham Jail,* p.75. Penguin Group.